TORTURE CENTRAL

TORTURE CENTRAL

E-MAILS FROM ABU GHRAIB

Michael Keller

iUniverse, Inc.
New York Lincoln Shanghai

TORTURE CENTRAL
E-MAILS FROM ABU GHRAIB

iUniverse books may be ordered through booksellers or by contacting:

iUniverse
2021 Pine Lake Road, Suite 100
Lincoln, NE 68512
www.iuniverse.com
1-800-Authors (1-800-288-4677)

ISBN: 978-0-595-45605-5 (pbk)

ISBN: 978-0-595-69589-8 (cloth)

ISBN: 978-0-595-89906-7 (ebk)

Printed in the United States of America

Contents

Introduction

In the months ahead, our patience will be one of our strengths—patience with the long waits that will result from tighter security, patience and understanding that it will take time to achieve our goals, patience in all the sacrifices that may come.

Today, those sacrifices are being made by members of our armed forces who now defend us so far from home, and by their proud and worried families …

I remember that moment. It was October 7, 2001. Emotions were still raw from the atrocities of the prior month, and our minds were swimming with the uncertainty of what lay ahead for our country—and the world. The time had come for us to respond, and the President of the United States was announcing our invasion of Afghanistan, the same nation that had humiliated a world superpower less than two decades prior.

A commander in chief sends America's sons and daughters into battle in a foreign land only after the greatest care and a lot of prayer.

We ask a lot of those who wear our uniform. We ask them to leave their loved ones, to travel great distances, to risk injury, even to be prepared to make the ultimate sacrifice of their lives …

As I listened to the President say those words, I remember turning my attention to my wife, Kendra, who was seated beside me on the couch in my living room, still giving her full focus to the nationally televised address. I thought back to her phone call four weeks earlier—the crack in her voice when she asked me if I had heard the news, that planes had flown into the World Trade Center. She was teaching her elementary school class at the time, and I was at work, behind a computer, writing some code for a client's web site.

They are dedicated. They are honorable. They represent the best of our country, and we are grateful.

To all the men and women in our military, every sailor, every soldier, every airman, every Coast Guardsman, every Marine, I say this: Your mission is defined.

The objectives are clear. Your goal is just. You have my full confidence, and you will have every tool you need to carry out your duty ...

I shifted my gaze around the room, taking stock of the things that I had been able to acquire in a relatively short time. I was twenty-three years old, it had been less than two years since I graduated college, married my wife, and started my first job; and here I was with a new house and a nice car—material possessions that most citizens of the world would be unable to acquire in a lifetime.

I recently received a touching letter that says a lot about the state of America in these difficult times, a letter from a fourth grade girl with a father in the military.

"As much as I don't want my dad to fight," she wrote, "I'm willing to give him to you."

This is a precious gift. The greatest she could give. This young girl knows what America is all about ...

The President's story made me ask myself: What sacrifices am *I* making for freedom? Why must this burden fall so heavily upon a fourth grader and her father, and leave me untouched? Why is it that those with less are always the ones left to sacrifice to protect the possessions of those with more? Am I the kind of man who, when my nation is reeling, will leave the fighting to others simply because I can, and because it's inconvenient to do otherwise? If I don't stand up now, how will I be able to live with myself?

Since September 11, an entire generation of young Americans has gained new understanding of the value of freedom and its cost and duty and its sacrifice.

The battle is now joined on many fronts. We will not waver, we will not tire, we will not falter, and we will not fail. Peace and freedom will prevail.

Thank you. May God continue to bless America.

One week later, I enlisted into the Florida Army National Guard. Less than three months later, I was on a bus headed to Army Basic Combat Training. The time had come for me to do my part.

◆ ◆ ◆

After returning from basic training, my life quickly fell back into its old routine—the only exception being that for one weekend a month, instead of using my time away from the office to do yard work or catch a movie, I would report to an armory just outside of Tampa, Florida, to participate in two days of military training; and instead of spending my annual two-week vacation on a cruise with my wife, I would convoy up to Ft. Stewart, Georgia, for training in my army occupation: MLRS artillery. Yes, for the next six years, until my term of enlistment was concluded, we would have to settle for short week-end cruises.

We were actually boarding one of those cruises the day U.S. troops invaded Iraq. We watched American tanks cross over the Iraqi border on a TV at a bar on the Promenade Deck. It was then we knew that it wasn't going to be a question of *if* I was called to war, but *when*.

But time stands still for no man, life marches on; and the years between my enlistment and my deployment were very active ones. I co-founded a software development company, which was a lot of work, but very gratifying; and in August 2004, Kendra gave birth to our daughter, Morgan.

It was just two weeks after my daughter came into the world that the first of four devastating hurricanes ravaged Florida. My unit was activated for disaster relief, so I spent most of the first two months of Morgan's life traversing the state, protecting gas stations from looting, directing traffic, and distributing ice and water.

In April 2005, about six months after wrapping up our disaster relief mission, word came that our orders were being prepared for a deployment to Iraq; we would be leaving in August for a sixteen-month tour. The exact mission—what we would be doing there—was yet to be determined. So I got my affairs in order. At work, we hired a couple of people to fill my position; I assigned power-of-attorney to my wife; and I put as many of the bills on auto-pay as I could.

August arrived right on schedule, and I reported to the armory for the two-week initial mobilization process, which was basically just a series of briefings, medical examinations, and lots of paperwork. On September 6, 2005, at 3:30 AM, my unit boarded a plane for Ft. Dix, New Jersey, to begin a newly devised nine-week army training program called SECFOR.

Our SECFOR training consisted of daily convoys and unmounted patrols through simulated Arab villages (populated by Iraqi contractors) constructed in the northeastern New Jersey woods. I also volunteered for and received additional training as a Combat Life Saver (CLS), where I learned how to administer IVs, insert nasal tubes, create field splints, control bleeding, establish triage, and various other medical skills necessary to keep a casualty alive on the battlefield.

With our training primarily revolving around convoy operations, I was surprised when we were informed—just prior to our overseas departure—that our mission in Iraq would be to conduct detainee operations at Abu Ghraib—a place made notorious the prior year when pictures of detainee abuse were published throughout the world.

Upon my arrival in the Middle East, I sent out an e-mail to my family and close personal friends to let them know I had arrived safely. Throughout my deployment, I would continue to keep in contact with them by sending periodic e-mail updates. I used these updates to describe my thoughts and feelings, my experiences, and my perceptions. What follows is a collection of those e-mails.

E-mails

11/22/2005
Greetings from Kuwait

Well I've arrived here on the other side of the planet. OPSEC (operational security) precludes me from giving out which base I'm at, how many people are here, or precisely when and how I'm leaving for Abu Ghraib (until I actually leave here). I can give you some vague descriptions—I'm about 15 miles from the Iraqi border in a designated "combat zone," and I'll be here for about 2 weeks.

The accommodations are OK. I sleep in a big tent with about 60 other guys (which has already developed a pungent odor). The weather has been good so far; and there is a decent PX, a Taco Bell, Burger King, Pizza Hut, and Baskin Robbins (decades ago who would have thought that a soldier would be buying a double scoop butter pecan waffle cone in the middle of a war—I don't know whether we can consider that progress or not, but it was tasty)—they are all inside of little trailers or tents, so it's not exactly like back home. The downsides are that there is very little personal space, the porta-johns are very poorly maintained, the Halliburton food at the DFAC leaves much to be desired, and everything is really spread out (for security against mortars/artillery). It's about a half-mile walk to the dining facility, and about a mile walk to the PX and fast food places; also we can't go anywhere by ourselves—so I have to find someone who is willing to go to the same place as I am, and stay until they are ready to go.

The flight went pretty well. We were on a chartered ATA 757. It took us about 16 hours with a 20-minute layover (to refuel and switch crews) in Ireland. I slept for all but about 4 hours of the trip. The last 30 minutes of the flight I was listening to some Cole Porter on my iPod, and I decided that for the last song before we land I'd just set it to shuffle and see which of the 600 some songs I had loaded would randomly come on. At that time the plane was starting its descent, and as the plane turned and the sands of the Middle East came into view I heard the distinct sound of Guns 'n' Roses, and I looked down on my iPod screen to see the song name: "Welcome to the Jungle." The song ended just as the wheels hit the ground.

I'm starting to get used to the idea of doing prisoner detention. I'm sure most of you know that I'm not real big on being the small cog in the big machine—I like for my work to be important, I like to be the essential indispensable ingredient. At first thought, prisoner detention seemed to be a rather unfulfilling mission, especially when compared to some of the other missions we could have drawn—like protecting U.S. Senators and Iraqi officials (VIP Security), protecting the transport of food and ammo and other necessary supplies (convoy security), or patrolling the streets to eliminate insurgents (route security). But once I started thinking of my job as not just "prisoner detention" but as "prison guard"—it started to take on a new meaning with me. My job is not just to keep the prisoner detained, but to also guard them from harm.

We've all seen the prisoner abuses that have taken place in Iraq. For some reason, the mainstream press has only focused on the more sensational prisoner humiliations (like putting panties on prisoners' heads, stacking prisoners in naked pyramids, etc.)—but prisoners have also been beaten to death in American custody. There have been actions by the U.S. Armed Forces and U.S. Intelligence Agencies that have made me ashamed of my country. I will now be in a position to eliminate any potential abuses in my area of operation, or to at least ensure that the methods put in place to stop such abuses are indeed working. I will be a one-man oversight committee (as I seem to be the only person in the company with any real concern for the detainees well-being)—which is right up my ally as I'm completely comfortable challenging "authority," and I have a very deep belief in human rights (which was one of the primary reasons I supported our overthrow of Saddam). So instead of defending my nation from terrorism by killing Zarqawi's al-Qaeda forces, I'll be defending my nation from terrorism by protecting us from ourselves, and that will hopefully make the detainees (many of whom are just innocent villagers picked up in big sweeps) less disposed to terrorism, and I can leave Iraq with fewer terrorists then there are today. So instead of killing terrorists with bullets, my weapon will be compassion … at least until snipers attack the ECP.

Hope everything is going well back home. Talk to you later.
Mike

11/26/2005
Kuwait Update—Day 6

Hello. Happy belated Thanksgiving. Not much is new here. On Wednesday we test fired our M-16s, M249 SAWs, and M-203 Grenade Launchers (to verify that they are all still in working condition). On Thursday we drove down to one of the other Camps here in Kuwait to have Thanksgiving dinner with the rest of our FL National Guard battalion (prior to deployment we were broken into three different companies with different missions throughout the theatre). Dinner was pretty good, no turkey but we did have prime rib and fried shrimp. Yesterday all NCOs attended a classified briefing on new technology which blocks the remote detonation of IEDs, then the rest of the company filed in for some additional IED training.

The physical environment of Kuwait is not quite what I had expected. We've done some traveling around (to a different camp, to ranges, etc.), and of what we've seen of the country so far—it is completely flat, no sand dunes (of course, all sand). With the exception of the army camps, I have seen no structures, no people, and no animals (not even insects). At night there is not a single star in the sky, it's completely black (with the exception of the moon). Looking out at night is reminiscent of being at the beach on a dark night, you see sand for the first 50 feet, then darkness all the way to the horizon. It also gets pretty chilly here—in the morning and evening I wear winter PTs, and I actually wore my poly-pro top (which is like a light-weight sweatshirt) during a couple of the afternoons. It's also really windy all of the time.

Since we have to go everywhere in pairs, I spend most of my time with SGT Greene. The two of us get along really well, we share the same sense of humor.

I finished reading "The World Is Flat" by Thomas Friedman. It's primarily about how technology has altered the global economy (and I highly recommend it to anyone interested in such matters)—but in one chapter he addresses terrorism (as it's a force that has great potential to cause a reversal in global business collaboration), here is an excerpt:

> Give young people a context where they can translate a positive imagination into reality, give them a context in which someone with a grievance can have it adjudicated in a court of law without having to bribe the judge with a goat, give them a context in which they can pursue an entrepreneurial idea and become the richest or the most creative or most respected people in their own country, no matter what their background, give them a context in which any complaint or idea can be published in the newspaper, give them a context in

> which anyone can run for office—and guess what? They usually don't want to blow up the world. They usually want to be part of it. A South Asian Muslim friend of mine once told me this story: His Indian Muslim family split in 1948, with half going to Pakistan and half staying in Mumbai. When he got older, he asked his father one day why the Indian half of the family seemed to be doing better than the Pakistani half. His father said to him, "Son, when a Muslim grows up in India and he sees a man living in a big mansion high on a hill, he says, 'Father, one day, I will be that man.' And when a Muslim grows up in Pakistan and sees a man living in a big mansion high on a hill, he says, 'Father, one day I will kill that man.'" When you have a pathway to be the Man or the Woman, you tend to focus on the path and on achieving your dreams. When you have no pathway, you tend to focus on your wrath and on nursing your memories.[1]

I'm not going to use these e-mails to espouse political ideology (after this one), but I thought that you might like to know why it is that I support this cause. I am not a man who is motivated by anger (over 9–11), hate (of Saddam and Osama) or fear (of terrorism and WMDs)—what motivates me is love (of freedom) and hope (in humanity). Unfortunately our political leadership has chosen to scare us with the former rather than inspire us by the later, which I believe is the main factor in the wavering public support for this war.

We are providing Iraq with the opportunity and the platform to create for themselves a pluralistic democratic society (a.k.a.,"the pathway")—a task that the Iraqi people were not strong enough to do on their own (and not for a lack of trying). America was in a very real sense responsible for the plight of the Iraqi people: we supplied Saddam with many of the weapons he used to suppress his people, and put billions of dollars into his pockets (which he used to prop up his regime) via our oil addiction. Many Americans seem to now believe that it's not our problem, or that creating a free Iraq—which has the potential to spread democracy throughout the region (as the American revolution did throughout Europe)—is not worth the blood we've spilled or the treasure we've spent in doing so, but if we continue to ignore the plight of the world's oppressed the problem will not go away, it will not improve, and desperate individuals will continue to be drawn to the bin Ladens of the world. Military force is rarely the appropriate solution, but sanctions, humanitarian aide, and UN Resolutions clearly weren't working in Iraq. Of course, this underscores the need for America to act properly (in the treatment of Iraqis, our own people, and others through-

1. Thomas L. Friedman, *The World Is Flat,* April 2005.

out the world), and set the example—so that we do not become the worlds biggest hypocrites. I know we are up to the challenge.

I've already had the opportunity to speak with over a dozen Iraqis (so far, all Kurdish and/or Shia), every single person that I ask is very optimistic about the possibility of success in their country, they expect a stable Western-style democracy in a matter of years (not decades)—and what I found most surprising is that there is very little ill-will toward the Sunnis (even after centuries of domination and recent years of domestic terrorism), there seems to be a genuine yearning for compromise and peace, which makes me proud to serve beside them.

Hope all is well back home. Talk to you later.
Mike

12/03/2005
Greetings from Iraq

Well, I've arrived in Abu Ghraib (henceforth referred to as Abu). The movement up here was an interesting and drawn out process. It started with us leaving Camp Behring (my duty station in Kuwait for about 10 days) via bus heading south. The bus ride lasted about two hours. When we arrived at the landing strip, we loaded all of our duffle bags on pallets and hopped on a C-130 for our flight into Baghdad. The flight was not very enjoyable—the plane didn't feel pressurized and the pilot engaged in evasive maneuvers prior to landing. The g-forces made it difficult to lift up your arms (or keep your head up), and the quick rolling back and forth made more than a few of us nearly loose our MRE lunch. It reminded me of a ride at the state fair called "Gravitron"—which is a room that spins at a high speed causing the centrifugal motion to press you up against the wall.

When the wheels came to a stop and our gear was slid out the back, we unbuckled ourselves and jumped out. As we were running off of the runway, the perimeter was attacked. So my first moments "in-country" I spent listening to a fire-fight. Through the shooting, I heard someone yell out "Welcome to Iraq"—I was glad to hear that someone had a sense for the dramatic. I guess we won the battle, because several minutes later the firing ceased. The security was pretty good—I was never in direct physical danger.

As we were preparing for our movement to Abu, it became clear that nobody was ready for us—for some reason they were expecting us to arrive on Sat 12/3 (not Wed 11/30), and there was no place available for us to stay. They scrambled and managed to find a few tents at Camp Stryker (10 minutes from the air field, 30 minutes from Abu), were we could bed down for a few days. Camp Stryker looks like something right out of the European Theatre in World War II—nothing like what I had expected or seen in any of my briefings. Our few days there were uneventful, a lot of free time, but not a lot of things to do (little phone/ internet access).

On Friday (12/2) evening we boarded a bus and headed to the helicopter pickup site for our final movement to Abu. A couple of hours before the chopper picked us up, as I was walking to the smoking area, I felt some blood trickle out of my nose. If it was caused by nerves, then the cigars I smoked (a Swiss brand which was surprisingly decent) must have doused them before they cropped to the surface, as I was completely calm and pretty relaxed throughout the movement (I actually laid on the ground next to the pickup site and got a little rest before our ride). The Chinook (a dual-propeller helicopter) picked us up just before midnight—since the last company to be dropped at our destination had been attacked with mortar and small-arms fire, they wanted us to fly in "under the cover of darkness."

The night before, at Camp Stryker, as I was lying in my sleeping bag, looking up at a moldy tent ceiling, listening to the sounds of gunfire and the occasional explosion from an enemy mortar round out in the distance, the thought occurred to me that "this is it, this is what its like to be in a war"—I had been waiting for some special feeling to alert me that this is real, but one had yet to come. As I prepared for a night chopper flight above Baghdad with a landing in a "hot" LZ, what I felt was an overwhelming sense of indifference. That night felt no different than the night before my flight to Ft. Dix, or the convoy to the FOB, or our flight to Kuwait, or our bus drive to Camp Virginia for Thanksgiving, or my C-130 flight into Baghdad.

I've always wondered what went through the mind of soldiers as they headed into danger. What was my great, great, great, great, great grandfather, Christopher Keller, thinking as he marched onto Long Island looking at British warships carrying thousands of troops that he would face musket-to-musket, or my great grandfather as he arrived in France during WWI, or my grandfather as he headed into the Pacific to evade Japanese Kamikazes in the second world war. I've always been a pretty even-keel, roll with the punches kind of guy, but the night before my big journey I really expected to feel something: nervousness, anticipation, apprehensiveness, excitement, fear, something. As the helicopter made its descent, and I arose from my rest, tightened up my IBA (body armor), put on my helmet, checked the rounds in my magazine, picked up my M-16, and donned my 60 lb. rucksack—I was about to get the "feeling" I'd been waiting for.

As soon as the Chinook's wheels touched down, I heard a voice behind me yell, "Move, Move, Move!" and the 30 of us who had lined up for the 3rd helicopter (my company moved in multiple birds, each leaving very quickly after the other) ran in an orderly single file line and filed into the back. As soon as the last man was in and buckled up, the gunner in the back threw up the door and we were up in the air. The flight over Baghdad was unreal—these things were tearing through the sky, and rolling and turning in what felt like quick, rapid motions. I was fortunate enough to be seated in front of a small window, and when I turned around, I saw the lights of the city swirling, and the chopper in front of us flying in the same wild manner. I thought to myself that it was like being on some extreme flying rollercoaster—the gunners that were around the bird wearing night vision and constantly scanning their sectors (in what appeared to be a frantic manner) help bring back the realization that this was not a pleasure ride—but when one of the Plant City boys seated next to me let out his best cowboy "whooooh"—I couldn't help but to smile.

When the wheels hit the ground, we quickly unbuckled ourselves, jumped out the back, and double-timed into the gates of our LSA at Abu. As I was exiting the bird, my mind flashed back to a game that I played when I was a boy: I'd jump off of my tree-fort with a plastic rifle and pretend that I was Rambo being dropped into a war zone. I may not be Rambo, but as I came off the helicopter I knew that this time I was doing it for real. The entire flight lasted less then 10 minutes—it was the coolest experience of my life.

12/03/2005
Pictures

I've attached a picture I took on our C-130 flight into Baghdad, and a picture of me in Camp Stryker. Unfortunately it was too dark (and it wasn't an appropriate time to use the flash) for any pictures on the Chinook.

12/05/2005
Iraq Update—Day 6

I've been in Abu for 3 days now, and I'm starting to get adjusted to my new surroundings. The camp is basically a bunch of abandoned/bombed out buildings surrounded by concrete walls and chain link fence. The buildings that were deemed salvageable (which basically means that the roof is not ready to cave in yet) were patched up with boards and plywood (though many still have gaping holes—and big burn marks are on almost every building)—and viola, here we are. It's a pretty dreary place—rubble and debris everywhere.

For about the next couple weeks or so we are being housed in what looks kind of like an old barn. When the unit that we're replacing leaves, we will move into the rooms that they vacate. The rooms are actually old Iraqi cells, they simply put plywood over the bars to give a degree of privacy. They were 2-man cells, but we are using them as 4-soldier rooms—so space will be really limited.

I believe that OPSEC prohibits me from giving details on the threat level and the number of attacks on the camp, but there are no civilian amenities: no McDonalds, Burger King, etc.—they all refuse to come here. At Camp Stryker, when I'd mention that I was headed to Abu, other soldiers would laugh and tell me "horror stories"—I thought they were just busting my chops, but now I see that their comments were accurate. Abu is rightly considered the worst Army camp in the entire world. When I say "no civilian amenities," I'm not exaggerating. There is not even an ATM machine, heck the Army won't even deliver the "Stars and Stripes" (our military newspaper) or put finance personnel here on post, and will only ship out packages for us once a week—the 3rd ID, out of the goodness of their hearts, bring some finance people by for a couple of hours every two weeks for us to withdraw cash from our checking accounts.

Everywhere we go, we are required to wear our IBA, Kevlar helmet, M-16, M-9 pistol, and a combat load of M-16 rounds (over 200) and 9 mm. rounds. The primary threats are insurgents who blindly shoot mortars over the wall (which accounts for a lot of the building damage), and snipers who go up some of the large buildings that are just on the other side of the outer walls (e.g., apartment buildings, a mosque, etc.) and shoot down at us. Guards have also been shanked by detainees, and car bombs have been driven into the ECP. That being said, the number of casualties "inside the wire" of the camp (where my job is) is relatively low, so it's good to be here in that regard.

On Saturday we did familiarization fire on the FM303, which is a brand new weapon they are deploying for prisoner detention. It's basically a paint-ball gun on steroids—instead of paint they can load the ammunition with O/C to squelch riots (which are pretty common). After that, we took a tour of the detention facility. Abu is not a prison in the traditional sense. Pretty much the entire detention area is outside. The vast majority of the detainees have communal type living in tents. So there will be a half a dozen army tents surrounded by a barbed wire fence and some razor wire, with guards walking around the perimeter, ensuring that all is well on the inside. Food is brought in, and the detainees feed themselves, shower themselves, etc. It's kind of similar to the POW facility in the movie "Hart's War" (or any other WWII movie about American POWs in Europe).

The detainees that need to be segregated are kept in the special housing unit (SHU), which is a row of 6 x 6 cells, still outside (with a roof over it). They kind of look like the cells in the "Pirates of the Caribbean" ride at Disney World. It's one detainee per cell; they get the "essentials": a bottle of water, a mat, a Koran, a blanket, etc.; but are prohibited from speaking for their entire stay at the SHU (which can last days or months). OPSEC precludes me from giving any more of a detailed description of the facility (e.g., number of prisoners, guards, etc.).

Yesterday we did a "shakedown" of one of the Level 1 compounds—compounds range from Level 1 (least dangerous) to Level 5 (most dangerous). I personally searched three tents (which includes going through everything: blankets, dirty clothes, trash, etc.) by hand. All I kept thinking the whole time was that I was going to end up walking out of there with body lice. When that was completed, we searched all of the detainees. I personally "patted-down" about 12–15 of them—sticking my hand down that many unbathed crotches was not a pleasant experience. I didn't find anything on their person, but I found all sorts of goodies in their tents: several shanks, hand-made brass knuckles, rock notes, and even a hand-carved club (with a sown-on cloth handle)—I can just imagine what they find in the higher level compounds here. It was a really gruesome process, and it took several hours (all afternoon). Guard shifts are 13 hours a day (either the day or night shift), and you work 9 days on, 1 day off.

Tomorrow we start on-the-job training with whatever specific detail (Level 1, 2, 3, etc.) that we are assigned. There is a chance that I will be assigned to S-6 (battalion signal)—which is basically maintaining the Internet service here at Abu—my command is aware of my civilian technical training and may make use of it.

Hope all is well back home. Talk to you later.
Mike

12/05/2005
Pictures—Day 6

I attached some pictures of Abu. I'm prohibited from photographing the detention area, but I can take pictures of the areas where we live.

The first picture is of the area where my company is currently staying. The second one was taken right outside the door—we are currently next to the LZ for the hospital that is on post, the Chinook was dropping off some casualties. The third one is of one of the other buildings here at Abu.

7120

12/08/2005
Iraq Update—Day 9

Hello. Well, so much for me "eliminate[ing] any potential [detainee] abuses." I've been assigned to S-6. More specifically, I've been tasked out to help maintain the in-room Internet service. I believe that Abu is the only facility in Iraq/ Afghanistan that provides in-room Internet for the soldiers' personal use. About a year ago, the battalion commander (who has since been rotated out with a new one), approved the idea to provide personal Internet service at the camp. They found a soldier who happened to have acquired the skills (via their civilian job) to establish such a network—and he proceeded to scrounge up any left over or unused equipment he could get from surrounding units to set it up. This facility is pretty large (280 acres), housing units are spread out, and since the rooms are former prison cells they were not built in a manner conducive to setting up such a system. So the network is a hodge-podge of really old equipment (a lot of junk rigged together); wires/hubs/routers/etc. are stuffed in any closet, baseboard, nook-and-cranny that he could find—run on roofs, draped over trees, etc.

Well, about a month ago—that soldier left, and was replaced by a new one who had just arrived and also happened to have computer networking skills. His name is SGT Ballou, he's my NCOIC (i.e., supervisor). Since he arrived on the scene he's been working to upgrade the equipment and redesign the network. Soldiers are charged $50/month to utilize the service, and he's using that money to buy new equipment and improve the quality of the system. He acquired his skills on the civilian side as well (as a hobby)—he's a self-described "tech-geek"—and he really seems to know his stuff. Since my command knew that I "worked with computers"—I've been assigned to assist him—so I'm the assistant network admin for the personal Internet service for the entire FOB of Abu Ghraib.

Up until now, pretty much all of my experience has been with software development—I really have very little technical knowledge of computer networking. However, I've really been wanting to get some experience on that side of the technology (so that I know the full-picture)—so I'm excited about having the opportunity to learn. I never really anticipated being assigned a job where I would actually enjoy the work. Though I spend a significant amount of time on the computer, it's not really a desk job. The system goes down multiple times a day (from soldiers messing with wires, old equipment failing, power outages, etc.)—which currently requires us to physically trace the wire (walk all over camp) with a lap-top, checking the routers/hubs/wires, to see which ones are down. Also, I have to take occasional convoys into Baghdad to pick up new equipment. It's a pretty busy job, people are constantly coming in with problems. My hours are pretty much 1300 to 0400 (15 hour days), 7 days a week (no days off).

SGT Ballou is about as non-military as you can get. He's in his early-mid 20s, spent a few years in active duty, did a tour in Afghanistan (where he worked as a radio operator), got out, signed a one year contract with the guard (to see how he'd like it)—and when his unit got activated, he volunteered to come along. The shop is just the two of us, since we're the only two people at the camp who really understand the technology—we are pretty much an island unto ourselves. All the higher-ranking know is that we're the "Internet-guys" who keep the service up. It really feels more like I'm at a small start-up tech company working out of a garage than it does a military assignment. It's a really relaxed and laid-back atmosphere.

Here at Abu, there are really only two things to do: work out at the gym, or surf the Internet. So when everything is up and working we are the most popular guys on post, and when things are down we are the most hated.

We're getting new satellite dishes at the end of the month, so it should be interesting setting those up. Also, a near-by unit is thinking about giving us some unused fiber-optic cable, so I may get the experience of laying that. The connection is currently pretty slow (less than dial-up)—so these enhancements should make a significant improvement in the quality of the service. Of course, it will be a lot of physical labor for the two of us. But even with the long hours, it's still a significantly better job than rolling around in the detainees' trash. I get to browse the Internet every day instead of browsing detainees' soiled groins.

For those interested, here is a link to some info on Abu: http://en.wikipedia.org/wiki/Abu_Ghraib_prison[2] [see Appendix A]

Hope all is well back home. Talk to you later.
Mike

12/08/2005
Pictures—Day 9

I attached a couple of pictures of the "office" where I spend most of my day.

2. "Abu Ghraib Prison," *Wikipedia.org*, December 2005.

12/14/2005
Iraq Update—Week 2

Well, I've completed my second week in Iraq—and some of the Iraqi people have treated us to some pre-election "fireworks." Abu was hit with a mortar round on Wednesday, and then a couple more on Thursday. I am pretty good at determining distance and type of weapons fire (i.e., M-16, .50 cal, AK-47, etc.) from the sound—but I have yet to acquired that skill with the insurgent artillery. The second mortar on Thursday made a thunderous boom which rattled my office—I don't know whether it was a small round that hit really close or a large round that hit somewhat close.

On Friday, a suicide bomber drove a VBIED (vehicle borne IED) up to a convoy exiting the Abu gates and detonated, killing one soldier and wounding eleven. I was running wire in a building about 100 meters from where it happened—it felt like the building I was in was hit (it was a large piece of artillery), so I went downstairs to see what was going on and I saw billowing black smoke rising from the other side of the wall. I was not in a position to assist, so I went back upstairs to finish my wiring job.

On Friday evening I turned in my M-16 to the arms room. It was getting too difficult to properly do my job (get into crawl spaces to run wire, etc.) lugging it around. I am still armed with my M-9 pistol—which is very effective at close range (about 100 feet).

On Saturday, I was involved in my first fire-fight. It was around 11 pm, and I was just locking the door to the office to go rewire one of the other buildings when I heard a ton of AK-47 fire—thousands of rounds. So I went back inside, grabbed my CLS (Combat Life Saver, a.k.a., small medic) bag—I thought I may need it. I started running toward the gate (the direction the fire was coming from). About 30 seconds into my run, the sirens started wailing (signifying an assault on the compound), so I shifted direction (as directed by SOP) and ran over to the closest Tactical Operations Center (TOC)—which was actually a different units command. By the time I arrived at the TOC (about 45 seconds after the first shots), the smell of gunpowder in the air was already overwhelming—I've spent days on gun ranges where tens of thousands of rounds had been expended and that odor did not approach this one. One of the Platoon Sergeants saw that I was a CLS (I don't believe there were any other CLSs or medics on site), and had me jump on the back of an up-armored 5-ton truck headed out towards the battle in a "reserve" capacity. Surprisingly during the ride into the action, I was consumed by a feeling of excitement. It was kind of like the feeling I used to have playing linebacker in high-school football, the moment I saw the quarterback roll to my side—giving me the opportunity to make a big play and deliver the big hit. Even at the time, I was consciously aware that I wasn't feeling even the slightest bit of fear—which is strange, a little fear can sometimes be beneficial—my only guess is that it's a result of the confidence I have in our comparative abilities.

When we arrived at our staging area, they took a count of us, and received a radio update of the situation while we triple-checked our ammo and prepared to move in. Then suddenly the shooting stopped—the heavy guns in the towers had destroyed the threat. After receiving the "stand-down" order, I headed over to my companies TOC to get an update from my unit. To my surprise, everyone in my unit was still in the barracks. I guess my units "leadership" decided to sit the battle out. Technically they didn't do anything wrong—all that's required is that after hearing the sirens they radio in where they are, and stand by for orders—but I would have liked to have seen someone else in my unit take some initiative instead of leaving the dirty work to others. I was the only soldier in my company that was in any way involved in the action—and I was only armed with a pistol.

What I noticed is that people respond in one of three different ways when the shooting starts:

1. They take the initiative, and run to the point of danger.
2. They stay with the crowd, doing no more or less than required.
3. They hang in the rear, shuffling their feet, leaving the heavy lifting to others.

I don't think anybody really knows how they're going to react until they are actually faced with that situation. Most of the people fell into the #2; they waited around for the siren and reported. The smallest group was #3, those who claimed not to hear the sirens, and found a proverbial hole to hide in. I was with one of the groups of soldiers who fell into #1, those who didn't wait for a siren, or for someone to force them to respond, but ran to engage the enemy and defend the camp. Quite honestly, I surprised myself. I was hoping to be a #2—to just do what was required—but my instincts kept pushing me forward, and I have complete trust in my instincts—they haven't failed me yet.

A few hours later, we were given some details on how the situation started. Apparently, a large mob of Iraqis in the pitch black night came running outside towards Abu and all opened fire. The guard towers, perceiving the possibility of an assault, returned fire with illumination rounds (to better see the situation), the

Iraqis then directed fire towards the towers—and the battle ensued. At the time, nobody was aware that the mob had initially ran outside and starting firing in celebration of an Iraqi soccer game victory. I don't know how many people have to die before they figure out its not a good idea to start firing thousands of rounds out of their assault rifles in the vicinity of a critical site army post—or figure out the difference between us firing flares and deadly rounds.

Surprisingly, we didn't suffer any casualties—I don't have a number for casualties on the Iraqi side. However later that evening, an Iraqi interpreter who lives at Abu was killed along with his son (he left Abu for the night to visit some relatives). MI (military intelligence) seems to think it may have been in "retaliation" for the incident.

My birthday was a quiet one—no attacks and business as usual.

Abu is being used for the elections—the building that my unit was sleeping in is actually being used as a polling station. So they moved us all out. Since there won't be any rooms available until the unit we are relieving moves out, my unit was moved into an already occupied building (the building with the Saddam painting I e-mailed last week) and set up cots in the hallway to sleep. I actually moved into the office instead. There is an improvised plywood wall separating the office from what used to be a different little office used for some admin—I moved my stuff into that abandoned office, and I am planning to live there for the remainder of my stay. It has more personal space than the cells that my unit will end up with—and a lot more privacy. SGT Ballou lives in another little room that's connected to the office—so it's just the two of us in here, and we each have our personal/private spaces.

On Friday, I was told that I had some packages, so I headed over to the mail room to pick them up. When the mail sergeant opened the door, I saw a huge mound of packages filling a whole corner of the room with my name on them—there were 14 of them. The mail sergeant just shook his head and said "Well, somebody sure loves you a whole lot." He had to find a Humvee so we could drive them back to my room—there was no way we could carry them all. I want to thank you all for your support. I am genuinely moved. Words really can't express how much it means to me. I wish there was something more that I could do from here to show my appreciation and gratitude. Thank you.

Mike

12/14/2005
Pictures—Week 2

I attached a picture of my room, and a picture of an up-armored 5-ton (they really should armor the back if they're going to use it to transport troops in a fire-fight).

43MPBDE96MP

12/16/2005
Iraq Update—Day 17

Yesterday was election day in Iraq. I am now officially living the world's newest democracy.

The detainees who haven't been convicted of a crime (which is virtually all of them here at Abu) had the right and the opportunity to vote. They voted a few days ago. The process was overseen by Iraqi election officials. One of the soldiers in my unit actually caught one of the election officials trying to stuff votes in the ballot box. The problem was resolved—I'm not sure what happened to the official.

As for election day violence, we had some shelling the night before (12/14) which was no big deal. Then that morning (12/15) we had an IED discovered that ended up blowing up four of our EOD (Explosive Ordnance Disposal) soldiers—they are all going to live. Two of the Iraqi guys who sell stuff here at Abu were also killed in separate incidents. But all-in-all, it was relatively quiet.

I had been wondering why the fire-fight on the night of 12/10 hadn't been reported in the paper. With the amount of rounds that our towers ended up firing, I'm sure that there had to be dozens of Iraqis killed and even more wounded, which to me at least seemed significant enough to warrant a blurb in the AP. So I asked one of my friends from my unit who had been assigned to S-2 (MI) what the official word was on the 12/10 incident (how many Iraqi deaths, etc.). He replied that according to MI, there were no outgoing rounds fired from Abu Ghraib therefore there couldn't be any Iraqi causalities caused by U.S. forces. I told him that I knew for a fact to be an incorrect assessment—and that I could provide sworn statements from soldiers who had witnessed boxes of .50-cal. rounds being fired from the towers. He said that he was aware of that—that at the guard briefing the next day when S-2 gave their official account, the room erupted in laughter at the absurdity—and that since there is no investigation into the matter, that no sworn statements are being accepted. Apparently, the Army is intent on keeping the words "Abu Ghraib" out of the news.

Now, before I deployed I would have expected that a reporter would surely catch wind of an event of this magnitude. However, since I've been in the Middle East, I have yet to see a single reporter, cameraman, news truck, or anything even resembling the media. Even the photographers, if you check out the name for AP photos (in publications where they actually give the name and not just list it as "AP")—you'll see that if it was taken in an unstable environment, the photographer usually has an Arabic name. The vast majority of reporters in the region stay locked up in the safety of their hotel rooms (just to get a "reporting from Baghdad" tag next to their name), and acquire the bulk of their information from briefings given to them by the military. So it's pretty safe to assume that the majority of the news you hear about Iraq is either military propaganda or blind conjecture from some miscellaneous reporter.

I also saw that a couple of days ago Bush estimated that the number of Iraqis killed since the invasion was around 30,000. About a week ago, I was talking to a guy who was a member of the 1st Marine Expeditionary Unit during the initial invasion into Iraq—he said that their unit alone took out about 10,000 (including 2 full sized brigade elements). So, that 30,000 number has got to be way off. I wouldn't be surprised if the real number had an extra zero at the end. With my personal experience, you can see how enemy casualties can easily go unrecorded.

I attached a picture of the plywood wall separating my room from the office—it may help give you guys a better idea of our layout.

Hope all is going well back home. Talk to you later.
Mike

12/20/2005
Iraq Update—Week 3

Well, I've now been in Iraq for 3 weeks, I've been in the Middle East for 1 month, and I've been federally activated for 4 months. This week has pretty much been more of the same: rewiring buildings, helping people with their PC problems, keeping the Internet service up, etc. We also had the usual couple of IEDs and some small arms fire—nothing major. I did get to brush up on some web design skills. I redid the AbuNet home page—nothing too exciting, but I think it's an improvement.

My job keeps me pretty busy. Since I've been here, we've ripped out about 12,000 feet of CAT5 and run about 5,000 feet of new wire—we've got about another 15,000 feet of new wire to go (and that's on top of the fiber optic we're going to run to replace our main trunk). Our network is pretty large. We have about 600 users, and around 400 individual rooms wired up in roughly 20 two-floor buildings over about a 2-mile area. We also have a dozen or so WiFi spots set up around the post. And all of this goes through our office, with SGT Ballou and I being the only two people working on the entire operation. On top of that, we also provide a help desk service to the soldiers here—it's not really officially part of the job, but there is no other place for these people to go with their problems. I'd say about half of the soldiers here are brand new to computers, having just purchased their first one for their deployment. So we hear a lot of questions, and have a lot of issues with users messing up their laptops.

But all of the work pays off when I see the face of a soldier right after we hook them up, enabling them to use their webcam to see their wife and children for the first time in weeks—sometimes they get very emotional. The service we provide is absolutely critical to the morale at this post, and I am baffled as to why the army refuses to spend a single cent on our operation. We are completely self-sustained by the $50/month fee that we charge the soldiers who utilize the service.

Before I arrived, SGT Ballou spent $3,000 out of his own pocket for equipment to get this place up and running (the previous network admin left it in an inoperable state)—he's anticipating that by the time we leave there may be enough left over in the account for him to recoup his money.

SGT Ballou and I work the longest hours on post by far—over 100 hrs a week (20 hrs a week more than the next closest job). Most of the soldiers here are appreciative of our work. Of course, we still get people in our office every day who cry about the connection speed or outages. I remind them that their subscription to the service is entirely voluntary and that I will give them a full refund at any time—but that they will never be able to re-subscribe to the service. I have yet to have someone take the refund, which lets me know that even the complainers are glad to have it. I'm planning on eventually coding a problem/question submission system, so that users can get assistance without having to come down to the office.

Most of the network problems we are dealing with are a result of wire breakage and loose connections (lots of wire that's been just taped together)—also we've got a bunch of cheap hubs (which we will be replacing with switches) that like to go out, periodic power-outages, and a bunch of users who like to unplug things and/or plug in their own devices.

Hope all is going well. Talk to you later.
Mike

12/20/2005
Pictures—Week 3

For those of you wondering how we receive small-arms fire inside of Abu, I attached a couple pictures of the outer wall. The buildings on the other side of the chain link are part of the surrounding neighborhood (which is predominantly hostile to our presence).

12/25/2005
Merry Christmas

Merry Christmas from Iraq

Sorry if Santa was late this morning, he was temporarily detained for possessing a suspicious bag.

12/27/2005
Iraq Update—Week 4

Well, another week down. I'm finally shaking off a cold that I acquired my third or fourth day at Abu. I think it's pretty much the result of being in a new environment—and one that isn't all too sanitary.

We have numerous Iraqis who live and work here at Abu. The Iraqi culture certainly has a different standard of hygiene. They also have a different method of using the toilet. Instead of sitting, they stand on the seat and squat over the hole. Sometimes their aim isn't very good and they make a mess of the seat, in one instance they didn't even bother to lift the lid. Soldiers have also gone into the showers to discover feces on the floor—I guess some think that the two-inch drain will suffice—needless to say, it doesn't. Because of these conditions a fair amount of soldiers stationed here contract dysentery.

I was talking to a soldier a few days ago who spent the first part of his deployment training the Iraqi Army. He had the same problem with the Iraqi troops making a mess of the latrines, causing a number of his soldiers to get ill, so he asked an Iraqi interpreter if he would talk to them about trying to be a little more careful. The interpreter went over to a group of them and yelled something at them, which caused the Iraqi troops to look embarrassed, then walked back and said that there would no longer be a problem with the latrines. When the soldier asked what it was that he said to them, the Iraqi interpreter replied: "I said, 'How do you expect to ever compare to the Americans when they can shoot a missile from the other side of the world and drop it into a window, and you cannot even drop your own shit into a hole between your boots?'"

Also, every person arrested throughout the entire country comes to Abu Ghraib for in-processing, brining with them just about every disease imaginable. A number of the soldiers whom we relieved are being quarantined at Ft. Dix for tuberculosis.

Whenever I step out of the office, the odor of this place hits me like a wave. The closest thing I can compare it to is the smell of old mildewy library books. I don't think it's a smell that I'll get used to. The flies/mosquitoes are also out in force.

I guess in every war troops come up with a little nickname for the enemy. We had the "lobster-backs" in the American Revolution, the "huns" in WWI, "charlie" in Vietnam, and this war is no different. The slang name used by American troops for Iraqis is hajji (pronounced ha-jE). In Arabic it means "enlightened one" or more specifically a Muslim who has made the pilgrimage to Mecca—so it's not technically an insult. However, it's not really being used in the proper connotation.

There are several Iraqis who have tables set up to sell stuff to the troops (mostly pirated and bootlegged DVD movies). Their tables are right outside of my room. Something that I've found odd is that these Iraqis all seem to have a real affinity for country music. They're not playing it for us, a lot of the guys in the immediate area are from Massachusetts, and some have asked them to please find a different genre to play—so far all requests have been denied. It seems like whenever I step outside I hear Alan Jackson on the radio. I've must have heard the song "Chattahoochee" about a 100 times since I've been here.

On Christmas Eve, I went to the table of the Iraqi who cells cigars to browse his selection. Buried among a pile of mediocre brands I found a hidden treasure: a Cuban Romeo y Julieta Romeo No 2. So on Christmas morning at about 3:30 am, I closed the shop up early, went outside, popped open a non-alcoholic beer, and enjoyed the first really good cigar that I've had since I've been here, while gazing up at the moon and the handful of stars that hang in the Iraqi sky. There was no sign of reindeer, but I did hear a chopper fly by—Santa Clause must switch out his sleigh for a Blackhawk when he gets to the Iraqi border.

I spent most of Christmas Day monitoring the network traffic to ensure that the rest of the soldiers had as much bandwidth as possible to communicate with their families, and watch their kids discover what Santa had brought them via their webcams. They didn't put on any sort of Christmas show here—understandably nobody really wants to come to Abu Ghraib—though I'm a little surprised that the post commander didn't try to put something together for the troops living here. We didn't get any of that steak and lobster I saw Rumsfeld doling out to the troops for Christmas dinner on CNN—we had pot roast.

I hope that everyone had a Merry Christmas. Talk to you later.
Mike

12/27/2005
Pictures—Week 4

I attached some pictures of my surroundings. If you look at that dark picture with the tables, that first red door on the left is the door to my room (in the back of our office). Those tables are the ones that the Iraqis set up to sell their DVDs.

If you walk down the hall to where it gets brighter, turn to the right, and take about six steps, you will be standing right where I took the attached picture of the motor pool.

01/03/2006
Iraq Update—Week 5

Well, another week has come and gone. I've had a few people ask about religion in Iraq, specifically how the Muslims react to our outwardly Christian celebrations and rituals (e.g., reading bibles, blasting Christmas music, statues of the nativity, etc.). From what I have seen, Islam in Iraq is pretty much just like Christianity in the United States. You have a majority who claim to believe in the faith (80% in America, 90% in Iraq), and many will wear the religious symbols (the cross in America, the headdress in Iraq), but most take the "word of God" with a grain of salt.

For example, in the bible, God himself commands things like: "If anyone curses his father or mother, he must be put to death" and "anyone who blasphemes the name of the LORD must be put to death"—but I'm sure you would find very few Christians in America who would support the death penalty for those actions. And under Koranic Law, alcohol consumption is "a great sin"—but I have yet to meet an Iraqi that doesn't drink.

From my perspective, Iraq is not a fundamentalist nation, and I have yet to speak to an Iraqi that would support a fundamentalist government. Generally, they seem to have a remarkable understanding of what "liberty" requires, as Thomas Paine put it: "He that would make his own liberty secure must guard even his enemy from oppression; for if he violates this duty, he establishes a precedent that will reach to himself." It seems that the vast majority does not want to replace a secular dictator with a theological one, or restrict the voice and rights of those in the minority. I would say at the present that the Christian Right has as much (if not more) influence in America as the Muslim Right does in Iraq.

The new Iraqi constitution—approved with almost 80% of the popular vote (try getting that for anything in America)—declares that "Iraqis are equal before the law without discrimination because of sex, ethnicity, nationality, origin, color, religion, sect, belief, opinion, or social or economic status; … followers of every religion and sect are free in the practice of their religious rites; … The state guarantees freedom of worship and the protection of its places. Every individual has freedom of thought and conscience." I think that's a pretty good start.

It's also important to remember that a substantial number Iraqis are Christian (3%)—which is significantly greater than the largest American religious minority (Jewish Americans comprise 1.3%). Their general feeling on the societal integration of faiths appears to be similar to Thomas Jefferson's: "It does me no injury for my neighbor to say there are twenty gods, or no god. It neither picks my pocket nor breaks my leg."

So no, I haven't seen any hostility towards the U.S. Army's Christian displays—I've actually seen several Iraqis walking around in Santa Clause hats, and heard one humming "Jingle Bells." Iraqis seem much more concerned with the other Muslims blowing them up than with the predominantly Christian Americans trying to provide security. Of course, my interaction with Iraqis has so far pretty much been limited to those with access to American posts—so it might not be a representative sample of the nation as a whole—but in our conversations I try to get not only their personal opinion but also their feel for the population as a whole and the different sects.

I watched the documentary "Voices of Iraq" the other day. It's a project where they distributed 150 video cameras across Iraq, and the Iraqis recorded their own thoughts, then passed them on to others to do the same, and so on (during the mid to later part of 2004). Many of the sentiments expressed in that video echoed views that I've heard from Iraqis that I've spoken to. It's worth checking out. Here's the website: http://www.voicesofiraq.com

It can be rented from NetFlix, or purchased here: http://www.mavgear.com/detail.aspx?ID=957

It's been pretty cold here lately—lows in the mid 30s; and most of my conscious hours are spent after the sun goes down, but I'll be glad to be working nights when the summer heat rolls around. I usually don't get to bed until after 0600, and sunset is around 1630.

They put together a little New Year's Eve party—with a "Las Vegas" theme, which was really just some Christmas lights strung up, a blackjack table where you could play with monopoly money, and some music. I arrived at the party on 12/31 at around 10:30 pm, and left about 15 minutes later. I found being at a New Years party without the people that I care about to be too depressing—but I appreciate the effort, it looked like quite a few soldiers were enjoying themselves.

It's pretty much been business as usual here. Of course we've had the usual snipers and small-arms fire, some IEDs, and mortars inside Abu—mortars pretty much sound like IEDs (actually mortar rounds are sometimes used as IEDs), the only difference being that depending on how close you are to where they hit, you can hear their impact with the ground.

There are speakers located outside of the dining facility (DFAC) that blast music throughout the area. The song selection is not what one would expect: Luther Vandross, Peter Cetera, Michael Bolton, etc. Hearing Aaron Neville's

"Don't Know Much (But I know I love you)" in the background—providing the soundtrack for a mortar attack is like something out of a Stanley Kubrick movie.

Since I've already described these types of attacks and experiences in the past, unless something changes, I'm not going to dwell on them in my e-mails. We haven't had anything requiring the alarms (or me to hop back into the 5-ton) since the night of December 10th. My office is right next to where we fire our outgoing artillery from (mostly illumination rounds)—so I'm constantly hearing big booms. It's all gotten pretty routine and mundane, though I'm still remaining focused and vigilant.

I hope that you all have a Happy New Year. Talk to you later.
Mike

01/03/2006
Pictures—Week 5

Living in Abu Ghraib feels a lot like living in an old Nazi concentration camp. Hundreds of thousands of Iraqis have been murdered and tortured at this facility (mostly "political dissidents"). It seems that everywhere you go here there is a reminder of the atrocities that occurred under Saddam Hussein: blood-stained floors (in some places, no amount of scrubbing can remove it), blood splattered walls, "drowning pools" (which we've filled in), improvised gallows, the list goes on and on; it's an eerie place.

I've attached a picture of an old crematorium (which is where several soldiers in my unit are housed), and of a bloody face print in that same room dating back to the Saddam days.

Here is a link to an interview from a former Abu Ghraib hangman to you may find interesting [see Appendix B]: http://www.telegraph.co.uk/news/main.jhtml?xml=%2Fnews%2F2004%2F05%2F02%2Fnbrit302.xml[3]

---

3. "Meet the real butcher of Abu Ghraib prison," *The Daily Telegraph*, January 2004.

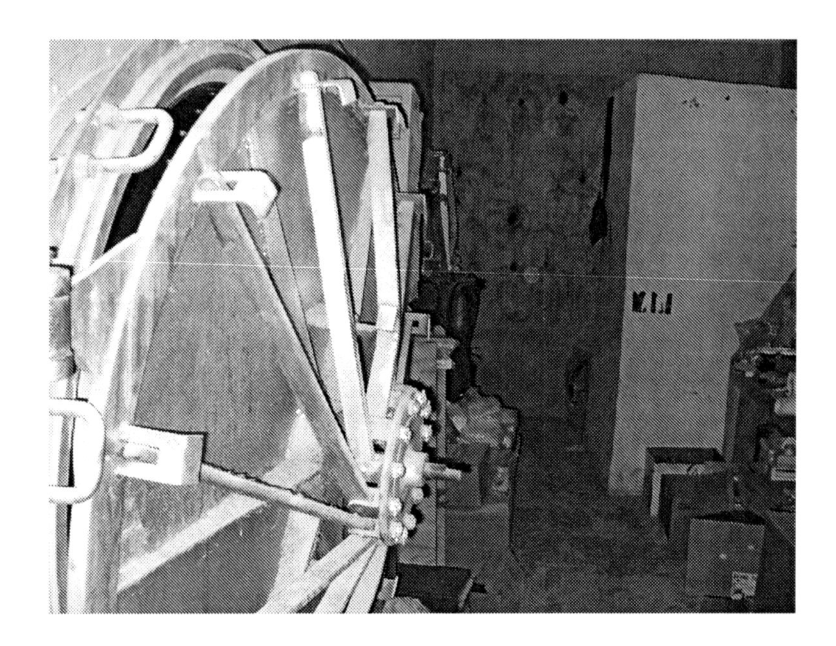

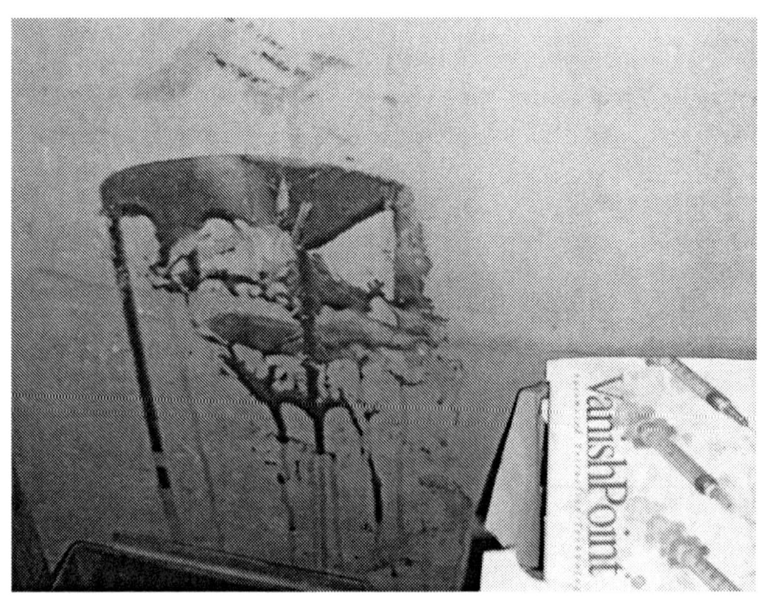
VanishPoint

01/10/2006
Iraq Update—Week 6

On New Years Day at 0400 during the daily morning headcount in one of the Level 1 tents, it was discovered that two detainees were missing. The alarms were sounded, the compound was searched, and a hole in the inner fence was detected along with several jackets laid across some of the concertina wire. A helicopter was mobilized, but there was no sign of the runaway detainees. Their escape attempt from Abu Ghraib was successful. There had only been one other successful attempt in the 18 months prior. I was waiting until it was reported by the press before addressing the issue in an e-mail, but it's been 10 days and I have yet to see it in any media publication.

I can't say that I blame the former detainees for escaping—I probably would have done the same thing if I were in their shoes. The fact that they were in Level 1 means that they probably hadn't done anything to warrant ever being detained.

Most of the detainees here have been captured by U.S. Marines, and the reasons for many of their detention is questionable at best. Here are a few of the reasons for the detention of some of our detainees here at Abu Ghraib:

* An anonymous tip was given that two employees from a cell phone company were supplying cell phones to insurgents. Marines went in and arrested all 20 employees.

* An Iraqi Police Lieutenant was driving in the opposite direction of a convoy—he waved and smiled at the Marines as he went by them. Several seconds later an IED exploded destroying both his vehicle and a Marine Humvee. The Marines arrested him for being in the area.

* A common one is for a neighbor to put in a tip that a certain individual is supporting the insurgency. Marines will go into the house and arrest everyone living there (which sometimes will be over a dozen people). Many times these tips are nothing more than disgruntled neighbors.

* A kid was kicking a soccer ball around with his friend. His friend kicked the ball too hard, it went past him and bounced in the direction of some Marines. The kid ran over to retrieve his ball and the Marines arrested him—I guess they didn't like him getting that close to them. Even his soccer ball is locked up in the personal affects area.

Could you imagine that one minute your child is in the front yard playing soccer, and the next he's just gone? Even if by some miracle you discover what happened to him, what comfort is there in knowing that he is being held indefinitely in a place notorious for inhumane treatment?

Once someone is detained in Abu Ghraib, the average time it takes for their case to be heard before the board (to determine whether they can be released) is 4 months—often it takes much longer. And then, even if it is determined that there is no need for their detention, they are not always released right away. In the case of the Iraqi Police Lieutenant, the board declared that his arrest was without merit over 9 months ago, and he is still here.

So what you have is a situation where the Marines are responsible for arresting the detainee, the Army is responsible for holding the detainee, and the Combined Review and Release Board (CRRB) is responsible for determining whether the detainee can be released. So the Army can blame the CRRB for not vetting the detainees in a timely manner, the CRRB can blame the Marines for detaining too many people, and the Marines can blame them both for having insufficient facilities and an inadequate process. This allows each party to be removed from the consequences/blame of the system—and of course leaves the detainees caught in the middle. The closest point of intersection between the three parties is the office of the Secretary of Defense.

The life of a detainee is not a very pleasant one. They're huddled together in tents, about 25 people per tent—which means that they have to sleep virtually on top of each other. The upside, for those living in Level 1 (the lowest security level), is that they are allowed to get as many blankets as they wish and they occasionally have access to a TV—I've heard that their favorite programs are "Tom and Jerry" and "The Lion King." Restrictions intensify as the security level escalates; Level 5 is the Special Housing Unit (SHU)—which is solitary confinement. There is also a tightly guarded hard-cell facility which is run by an entirely different unit (which even I don't have access to).

I had one guard tell me that a detainee said to him: "Before, me no problem with America. But now when I leave, I do very bad things." Personally, I fail to see how a policy which breeds that level of resentment is helping to win "hearts and minds."

I came across a small link to this article a couple of weeks ago: http://www.washingtontimes.com/national/20051223-121235-3444r.htm[4]

How much training do they believe is required for soldiers to know that it's not appropriate to beat shackled detainees to death (on multiple occasions)? And if the problem really is due to a lack of training, who is going to be held accountable for it?

And this isn't just an isolated incident, plenty of others can be found throughout different media publications (for some reason, usually buried in the back pages). Here's another one—tortured to death over two years ago and nobody has been charged: http://www.time.com/time/magazine/article/0,9171,1129601,00.html[5]

I guess we are citizens of a nation whose policy is to torture and murder with impunity. At least when Saddam did it, he didn't claim it was in the name of liberty and democracy.

On Saturday it rained for the first time since we've been here. It poured for a good part of the day, needless to say, everything is flooded. The ground is still completely mud (three days later)—everywhere—most areas it's between 8 to 12 inches deep.

Hope everything is going well back home. Talk to you later.
Mike

01/10/2006
Pictures—Week 6

Since I have been unable to procure a copy of the Abu Ghraib Standing Operating Procedure (SOP)—which is a whole other story in itself—the special OPSEC rules governing pictures at Abu are not entirely clear. However, I've received verbal confirmation that though we are not permitted to have pictures of the detainees, we are allowed to have pictures of the detention facility. So here they are. These are all of the Level 2 facility (though Levels 1, 3, and 4 look similar).

4. Rowan Scarborough, "Senior prison officer cleared," *Washington Times*, December 2005. Reports that an army officer charged in connection with the 2002 beating death of two detainees has been cleared of wrongdoing. The decision was based on the opinion that his unit received inadequate training prior to deployment.
5. Adam Zagorin, "Haunted by 'The Iceman'," *Time*, November 2005. Tells of a detainee who was killed during an interrogation at Abu Ghraib in 2003. The corpse was iced down and smuggled out of the facility in a blanket to avoid discovery.

01/17/2006
Iraq Update—Week 7

I had planned on going to bed early on Wednesday night, but it rained pretty hard (again) for about an hour that evening which caused some problems with the network—so I didn't end up getting to sleep until the usual time, 0600. Two hours later, I was crawling out of bed preparing myself for my first convoy through Baghdad. At 0900 my up-armored Humvee rolled out of the gates of Abu Ghraib.

So there I was, a computer programmer from Tampa, Florida, in the turret of a gun truck, manning an M249 SAW, headed down one of the most notorious roads in the world—a stretch of MSR commonly known as "IED Alley." When I pulled back the charging handle of my SAW, positioning the first bullet of the 200-round box of ammunition into the weapons chamber, the grogginess that I had been feeling instantly evaporated—I seemed to have a heightened level of alertness. With all of the training I had received on how to perform the duty of Humvee Gunner, I felt well prepared—and with the 4 extra boxes of ammunition at my feet, I was well armed.

SGT Ballou was my driver, and it was just the two of us in the vehicle. OPSEC prohibits me from giving the number of vehicles in the convoy. The purpose of our trip was to pick up three satellite dishes that we had shipped from the U.S.

The outskirts of Baghdad defy the common stereotype. There is a lot of greenery and ample brush—making many environmentally advantageous positions to place an IED or to launch an ambush. There was plenty of farm land, cows and sheep grazing in the pasture, and small houses. There were also a couple of dozen children who would run up to the road as we drove by to wave to us throughout various portions of our journey. From S-2 (military intelligence) briefings, I was aware that insurgent attacks are less likely if children are present (many insurgents have children and operate in their own neighborhood, and they do not want their own children caught in the cross-fire)—so I was glad to see them (plus they were pretty adorable). Sure enough, we reached our destination unscathed. We then broke away from our convoy, and headed out on our own to pick up our equipment.

When we arrived at the warehouse holding our satellite dishes, before they would allow us to leave with our stuff, they notified us that we first had to go to the customs office to acquire the proper paperwork. Luckily it was only about a half a mile away and on a secured road, making it an easy drive. The whole process at the customs office worked like this: we would see one person and explain to them the purpose of our being there, they would scribble some Arabic words on a piece of paper, collect a "fee," and give us directions to the office of the next person we needed to see. This happened about 5 or 6 times, and on a couple of occasions we also had to drive back and forth to the warehouse to get some additional documentation that they required.

For those concerned about equal professional opportunities for the women of Iraq, you'll be pleased to know that the person in charge of the customs operation was a woman. You may ask how it is that I know that she, in fact, was in charge. Well the answer is simple: she had her own office, she was the final person we had to see, and she received the largest "fee:" $350 (U.S.).

At one point I contemplated just pulling out my 9 mm. berretta and forcing them to load my equipment at gunpoint. Since I wasn't on a U.S. post I probably could have gotten away with it, and since their behavior was nothing less than extortion I would have been justified, but I didn't think that it would help with the whole hearts and minds thing, and I'm figuring that the we should have enough left over from everyone's monthly $50 to reimburse me this month. Finally after exhausting the cash that we had on us, they let us leave with our equipment, though all of the running around caused us to miss our scheduled time to link back up with the rest of our convoy—so we had to spend the night at the nearest post, Camp Liberty.

Being at Camp Liberty reminded me of just how good most of the soldiers deployed to Iraq really have it. It's actually kind of pretty there, plenty of palm trees, palaces, and big lakes. They have Pizza Hut, Burger King, Subway, a PX (actually multiple PXs, some resembling Wal-Mart), a movie theatre, a convenience store, a library, Internet cafes, TV lounges, etc. All there every day, whenever the soldiers want it. At Abu the only food available is the Army DFAC, and the only entertainment is the Internet service provided by SGT Ballou and myself. If they could just swing by Abu with one Big Mac a month for us it would really make a big difference—oh well, it could always be worse.

Since we hadn't planned on spending the night, we didn't have any of our sleeping gear. We ended up crashing on a couple of couches in some miscellaneous lounge for a little nap, and then watching some DVDs. At 0600 Friday morning, we linked up with another convoy headed to Abu. This time I drove (with Ballou riding in the passenger seat). It was really foggy that morning, I could barely see past the hood of my Humvee. With visibility that limited, it's kind of like a leap of faith—you just step on the gas, keep it on the road, cross your fingers, and hope that you don't get blown up—and fortunately we didn't. The convoy that we had missed on Thursday evening did encounter an IED.

We spent Friday night, Saturday, and Sunday setting up the new satellite dishes. They are now completely integrated into the system—boosting our speed close to dial-up.

As far as attacks on Abu Ghraib are concerned, violence has seemed to pick up slightly—with the action being a little bit more bold. We've had an increase in daytime small arms attacks, which I actually consider good news. Looking at it strategically, a small arms attack on a position like Abu Ghraib is pretty ineffective. Unless the attack is coordinated with some sort of artillery, the casualties are going to be very lopsided in our favor. This implies to me that other more effective methods (such as mortars, IEDs, suicide bombers) aren't as available—whether it be due to a lack of equipment or skilled personnel.

But I am still aware that our adversary is a devious one. Here is the latest example of their cunning: http://www.sundaymirror.co.uk/news/tm_objectid=16559740%26method =full%26siteid=62484%26headline=hiv%2dbombers%2d-name_page.html[6]

The British seem to be taking this new threat very seriously—even issuing new equipment for their troops to limit the risk.

For those of you who may be stressed by my deployment, don't worry, the Pentagon has a solution that should solve all of your problems: http://www.usatoday.com/news/washington/2006-01-12-pentagon-laughter_x.htm[7]

It reminds me of one of SNLs "Deep Thoughts:" "Dad always thought laughter was the best medicine, which I guess is why several of us died of tuberculosis."

Hope all is well. Talk to you later.
Mike

---

6. Rupert Hamer, "HIV Bombers," *Sunday Mirror*, January 2006. The article describes an al-Qaeda tactic to recruit HIV+ people as suicide bombers in the attempt to infect nearby coalition soldiers who are outside of the bombs normal kill range.
7. Gregg Zoroya, "Pentagon to families: Go ahead, laugh," *USA Today*, January 2006. Reports on a new Pentagon program that teaches the families of deployed soldiers how to "walk like a penguin" and "laugh for no reason" as a way of coping with stress.

01/17/2006
Pictures—Week 7

Since I was preoccupied with security during my convoy, I was unable to take any aimed photographs. However, I did wedge my camera into a groove in the bottom of the turret, and periodically while I was scanning, I would reach down and press the button—and it took a picture of whatever happened to be in front of it. A few of them turned out alright, I attached two of them.

I also attached a picture of some up-armored Humvees, and a picture of SGT Ballou on his laptop while we were working on one of our new satellite dishes.

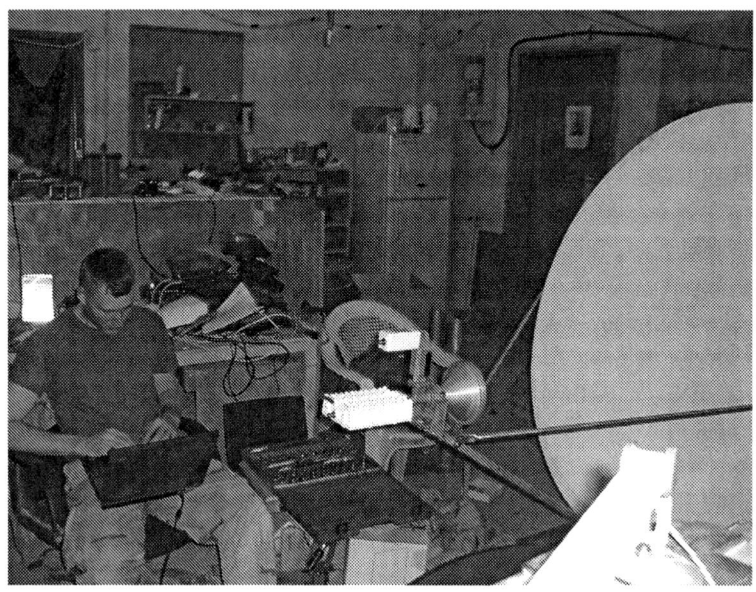

01/24/2006
Iraq Update—Week 8

On Wednesday, the side of our office was hit by a mortar. Neither SGT Ballou or myself were injured, and we only had one minor piece of equipment damage. A new unit had arrived two days prior, and a building next to them was hit as well—they were pretty freaked out by it. I don't think it will take them long to get used to life here at Abu Ghraib.

I moved into a new room. It's about 40 ft. down the hall from the office. Since Ballou has irregular sleeping patterns—and is often awake while I'm asleep (and vice-versa)—being in a more secluded single room is more convenient.

Most of the mud has finally dried up—so that makes life here a little more bearable. Not much else is new, so I'll just share some thoughts and a couple of anecdotes:

I've heard it said that the members of the U.S. Armed Forces here in Iraq are representatives of the United States, but it's really much more than that. The average Iraqi has never heard of Thomas Jefferson or Martin Luther King, they know nothing about our Bill of Rights, and they don't hear our president's speeches. The only real knowledge they have of America is from their interaction with U.S. Soldiers and Marines. If we are abusive, then to them America is a cruel nation. If we are just, then America is benevolent. To them, the members of the Armed Forces ARE the United States. To be the living personification of something that I love so much is an enormous responsibility—I don't believe that any person is fully capable of the task. But I wake up every day and give it my absolute best effort, and hopefully that will get me close enough to the objective, so that one day I can look back and be proud of my service here.

I was IM-ing one of my friends back in the states the other day, and he mentioned that he believes the reason why many returning soldiers don't talk about their war-time experience is because they know that people who were never in this environment would be disgusted by it (i.e., "you wouldn't understand").

I agree with his assessment completely. It seems that as you see people get killed and maimed, and with your life in perpetual danger, your mindset tends to shift, and things that you would normally find repulsive somehow become humorous and amusing. I think it may be a natural coping mechanism that the human mind has—that this isn't really real, that we're just a part of some big dark comedy.

For example, there is an insurgent fighter who is being detained here who suffered a gun-shot wound to his side (from a previous battle) several months before he was captured. Because the wound had gone so long without being properly treated, he is left with a permanent deep hole in his side. He was issued a wheelchair, and medics come in and plug the hole up with fresh gauze every couple of days. Well, the other day, some of the guards found him lying in a tent, pretty beaten up, and sobbing inconsolably. They took him to the medics, and there he disclosed that four of the other detainees knocked him out of his wheelchair, held him down, pulled out his gauze, and took turns gang-raping the hole in his side. The medics had some difficulty pumping the other guys fluids out of him, and it caused such a bad infection that he almost died. I'm sure that you all probably find that repulsive—it had us laughing for hours. Returning soldiers leave stories untold because nobody wants to come home and have people think that they are a monster for getting through the days by finding pleasure in other peoples pain—some may even feel guilty about it after leaving this environment and reverting back to their normal lifestyle.

There are soldiers who have stories like that intertwined throughout their whole experience—I don't blame them for wanting to keep it to themselves. I was actually a little apprehensive about discussing this issue, but one of the reasons I write these e-mails is to try to give you guys an idea of what its like here, and I wouldn't be doing a very good job of that if I didn't mention this subject. However now that this topic has been properly addressed, I probably wont be sharing any more of these types of stories, either.

And now one you might find amusing:

One of the Iraqi vendors outside of my door will occasionally put cultural items on his table: headdresses, hookah pipes, lanterns, etc. Well a few weeks ago, I saw one of the soldiers in my unit leaving the guys table with armfuls of Iraqi currency—the old stuff with Saddam Hussein printed on it. He must have had about $300 U.S. dollars worth. So I stopped and asked him what he was planning to do with it all. He replied: "Hey Sergeant, haven't you ever heard of investing in others peoples money? You know where you buy some others country's money and in a few years it's worth more?" I replied that I am familiar with foreign currency speculation, but unfortunately what he just purchased are the old Iraqi dinars which were disendorsed by the Iraqi government over a year ago. He then asked: "So you don't think that I'm going to make any money off of it? I bought every dollar he had!" I told him that his newly bought money is completely worthless, the guy was just selling it as a souvenir because some people think it's cool to have bills with Saddam's face on it. So the soldier went back and tried to get a refund, but of course the Iraqi wasn't going to give him his money back. I felt bad, and bought $30 U.S. dollars worth off of him. I'll give some out to you guys when I get back.

Hope everything is going well back home. Talk to you later.
Mike

01/24/2006
Pictures—Week 8

Here are a couple more pictures taken during the convoy last week. The first one is of a mosque.

01/31/2006
Iraq Update—Week 9

NOTE: While there is no classified information in this e-mail, the Uniform Code of Military Justice (UCMJ) is unclear as to whether making PUBLIC statements critical of ones chain of command is permissible. Since there are statements that some may erroneously construe as being critical of my chain of command, to be on the safe side, this e-mail is personal, private correspondence between myself and close friends and family members. I have also redacted the names of the people, unit, and location. DO NOT FORWARD THIS E-MAIL TO ANYONE FOR ANY REASON.

It was apparent since my arrival here that there were several inconsistencies between provisions specified in the Geneva Convention and the actual treatment of detainees. I voiced my concern in a letter to my Company Commander, and then later to my Battalion Commander (both of which are attached to this e-mail). [see Appendix C and Appendix D]

Here's a link to a *NewsWeek* article (published in November) that has a picture of a restraint chair that was typical of the kind used here and referenced in my letters [see Appendix E]: http://www.msnbc.msn.com/id/10020629/site/newsweek/[8]

One item that I was particularly concerned with was the use of medical litters (a.k.a., stretchers) in the Special Housing Unit (SHU). Medical litters were designed with the intent that they be used to transport the wounded. But here, one of their primary uses was to inflict pain and suffering on detainees for the purpose of punishing them for committing disciplinary infractions. I've attached a picture of former Army SSG Ivan Frederick (referenced in my letters) sitting on a detainee in double litters. [see Appendix F]

This procedure was described by some of the soldiers who work in the SHU and administered the punishment as follows:

If a guard desires to inflict this punishment on the detainee, he first radios in a request for approval from the Sergeant of the Guard (SOG). The SOG gives approval verbally over the radio—he is not required (nor does he in practice) physically go to the SHU. None of the guards with whom I spoke could remem-

8. Evan Thomas and Michael Hirsh, "The Debate Over Torture," *Newsweek*, November 2005. The article describes enhanced interrogation techniques used by America in the war on terror that have been dubbed "torture-lite"—including tactics such as stress-positions and sensory deprivation. The value and appropriateness of these techniques are being debated by members of Congress and the military.

ber a request for this procedure ever being denied. The detainee is then laid flat on a medical litter, and another litter is placed on top of them (producing a sandwich effect). The two litters are then tightened together with ratchet straps, creating a vice. The detainee remains crushed between the litters for one hour, with the guard checking every 15 minutes to ensure that the detainees still has a pulse. If after one hour, the guard still desires to keep the detainee between the litters, they again request radio approval from the SOG, and the process is continued. A typical reason for extension is a detainee trying to speak while being compressed. Defecating on oneself is one of the most common causes for a detainee to be punished in this manner (though latrines are not provided in any of the cells in the SHU, and guards do not always respond to latrine requests in a timely manner). Using medical litters to disciple detainees was routine practice in the SHU for at least a year (probably longer)—and by the previous unit/battalion that ran the facility as well. It was performed multiple times a week.

I put my concerns in a letter which I delivered to my Company Commander on 12/21. After receiving no response, I wrote a letter to my Battalion Commander and delivered it to her office on 12/28.

On 12/29, my Battalion Commander went into the SHU and directed that restraint chairs and medical litters no longer be used to punish detainees. My letters were then handed over to the magistrate's office for an investigation.

On 12/30, my Battalion Commander went to my First Sergeant and demanded that I receive "corrective action" (a.k.a. punishment, such as: demotion in rank, fined a month's pay, extra-duty, etc.) for "skipping my chain of command" by addressing my letter to her. My First Sergeant replied that I hadn't skipped my chain of command (I had written my Company Commander first), that he didn't believe that I had done anything to warrant correction action, and that he wasn't going to impose any on me. He did, however, strongly suggest to me that I drop the matter.

I guess my Battalion Commander didn't have the audacity to administer the corrective action herself, because I have yet to receive any. All accounts were that she "went ballistic" and was enraged at my actions—apparently even though she is the one in charge, she didn't want me to address this issue with her (or at all).

My First Sergeant deserves credit for standing up and going to bat for one of his troops in the face of an immoral (and potentially illegal) order from a "superior" officer. Though if corrective action were imposed, I would have objected and taken a court-martial—I wasn't going to be intimidated or deterred.

Everything in my letter was well known throughout the post, by those working both inside and outside of the compounds, and was proper procedure as dictated by the chain of command. It seems odd that a letter mentioning things that everybody already knew about would receive such a charged reaction (the fact that many of these practices were detailed in *Newsweek* a month prior further demonstrates that it was common knowledge)—but it did.

Anyway, I persisted, making it clear that I was willing to take this issue as far as it needed to go to be resolved, and since medical litters and restraint chairs were no longer being used, I felt that real progress was being made.

On 1/5, I heard that my Battalion Commander was relieved of her command over of the detention facilities (though she is still Battalion Commander), with the Post Commander taking control of that position. I'm sure that the detainee escape (which still hasn't been reported by the press) played a large role in that decision.

On 1/9, the commanders of each company in the battalion were given a copy of the Standing Operating Procedure (SOP), with the instructions that it be posted in their respective TOCs for soldiers to review at their convenience.

On 1/10, I received a copy of the SOP. I noticed that there were numerous amendments dated 12/28/05 (yet the "date modified" of the files were actually 1/4/06) which corrected the issues that I had addressed in my letter—effectively resolving the problems.

The only reason that I can think of as for why these problems existed for so long is that there is a culture of intimidation in the military, which is established from day one with the Drill Sergeants at Basic Training—you don't question what you're told, period. The desired result being that when a soldier is confronted with physical danger he is rambo, but when faced with a moral dilemma he becomes milquetoast—sometimes I get the impression that more value is actually placed on the latter. This timidness seems to also permeate the upper levels of the chain of command.

My questioning of our policies angered the Lieutenant Colonel to the point that she wanted me punished. Rocking the boat can make your life extremely difficult. This story of a recently passed veteran further demonstrates that point: http://www.usatoday.com/news/opinion/editorials/2006-01-12-thompson-edit_x.htm[9]

---

9. "A Hero Scorned," *USA Today*, January 2006. Tells the story of Hugh Tompson, a helicopter pilot during the Vietnam War who ended the My Lai massacre. He returned home to threats, harassment, and insults from those in his community and members of Congress.

Also we are trained that these people are the enemy. Every day Iraqis are trying to kill us: with mortars, IEDs, snipers, etc. It's hard for the soldiers to have any sympathy at all for them.

The environment here is completely different. It's like living in the wild west or something—the normal rules don't seem to apply. For example, here we kill people for driving too close to us, so I guess soldiers figure what's the big deal about a restraint chair or double litters, after all 'its still a lot better than what Saddam was doing to them.' I'm sure that the altered mindset I described in last weeks e-mail is also a big factor.

And where is the Red Cross? Under the Geneva Conventions, they are obligated to monitor these facilities to ensure that the rights of the detainees are not being violated. I've been here over two months and have yet to see any of their representatives. I've talked to soldiers who have been here over 6 months, and they've told me that during their time here, nobody from the Red Cross (or Red Crescent) has ever bothered to show up to inspect the compounds.

Nobody would stop Teddy Kennedy, Hillary Clinton, or any other member of Congress from checking this place out either if they so desired. It seems that everyone is quick to score political points by criticizing the Bush Administration for the handling of detainees, but nobody is willing to actually roll up their sleeves and go to work to ensure that everything here is copasetic.

Plus, there seems to be very little pressure from the citizens of the United States to end these practices. Articles like the one in *Newsweek* are published and nobody bats an eye. Heck, a poll referenced in that article shows that 58% of Americans actually support torture. I remember in middle school reading *The Diary of Anne Frank*, wondering how so many German citizens could be complicit in the face of the holocaust—but I guess when people feel that their life is in danger (whether it be by the allied powers or terrorists) they will rationalize and justify just about anything. Or maybe for some it's just like Jack Nicholson's character said in *A Few Good Men*, they can't "handle the truth"—they just don't want to know what's going on, they'd rather look the other way, depend on the govt. to "protect them," and pretend that ignorance somehow keeps their hands clean and their conscience clear.

But ultimately, there is no excuse for torture—even if its called "torture-lite"—and it really shouldn't have required a couple of letters from me (bringing the possibility that some mid to high level officers would be exposed) to correct the problems.

If our govt. was serious about eliminating this type of behavior everywhere, they would set up some sort of avenue for soldiers to report potential problems.

Something outside of the military chain of command (where there is a fear of reprisal)—something like a phone number for the Dept of Defense (or a Congressional Committee) that could be called anonymously.

But I'm glad that I've been able to contribute to the end of "torture-lite" here. It's another example that one person can make a difference.

Hope all is well back home. Talk to you later.

01/31/2006
Pictures—Week 9

I've attached some more pictures of Abu Ghraib.

The first one is a night picture taken of a section of a wall that partly covers my LSA, including one of the many old guard towers that are located throughout this place. They were used when Abu was still under the control of Saddam Hussein to keep overwatch of the hard-cell facilities—which are now being used to house the soldiers stationed here.

The second picture is of our battalion headquarters.

The third picture is of me on the roof of our office (where the satellite dishes are set up).

The fourth picture shows part of a mosque on the other side of one of Abu's outer walls.

It rained again pretty hard on Wednesday, so all of the mud is back.

DANGER

02/07/2006
Iraq Update—Week 10

The most common question that I get is about the food here at Abu. I eat the dinner chow (17:00–19:30) and sometimes the midnight chow (23:00–01:00). Occasionally they will serve a decent meal, but usually the quality of the food ranges from fair to inedible (think high school cafeteria caliber). Thankfully they usually have cold-cuts available at the dinner chow, so on really bad days I can just make myself a swiss-cheese sandwich (and enjoy the care-packages you guys send). For this service, the Department of Defense pays KBR (a subsidiary of Halliburton) $18 per meal per soldier. KBR/Halliburton must be making money hand-over-fist in the place. The list of services that they rape the American taxpayer for is so bad that it's almost comical.

My personal favorite is that we pay KBR, who turns around and pays local Iraqis, to come on post and literally throw water on the ground. It's a hilarious thing to watch. These guys walk around with a bucket full of water and a little cup. They dip the cup into the bucket, and with all of their strength slam the contents of the cup onto the ground. It's not intended to clean the ground or anything (its not soapy water), and they don't have a mop. I think the official rationale is that it supposedly keeps dust out of the air—in reality it's just a useless activity.

There are also a couple KBR teams that go around camp sweeping the desert sand—not the concrete floors—the actual ground in-between the buildings. They spend all day just pushing sand back and forth from one place to another. I have no idea what the rationale of that activity is—but I'm sure we're paying a pretty penny for it.

Here's a story I came across that, if true, I find particularly reprehensible: http://www.halliburtonwatch.org/news/contamination.html[10] [see Appendix G]

(FYI, while bottled water is available for drinking, KBR water is used for everything else: handwashing, showers, brushing teeth, often used in coffee, etc. Since Senate Republicans refuse to investigate, the Senate Democratic Policy Committee took it upon themselves to review the drinking water matter—unfortunately they don't really have the power to do anything about it.)

Halliburton/KBR is under a cost-plus contract, meaning they are reimbursed for all of their costs, plus they are then paid a percentage of those costs as a fee (for their profit). So they're actually incentivized to make the costs as high as possible (i.e., waste money). Additional abuses caused by this policy are well documented and easy to find online (one of the most outrageous is that, reportedly,

---

10. "Whistleblowers' stomach-curdling story," *HalliburtonWatch.org*, September 2005.

$80,000 trucks are routinely abandoned/torched if they acquire a flat tire or need an oil change). Of course, you've all probably heard about them pricing the cost at $2 per can of soda and $100 per laundry bag washed for each soldier. Since it's a no-bid contract, they don't have to worry about a competitor offering the same services for a lower price.

Consequently, 2005 was the most profitable year in Halliburton's 86-year history, with their govt. contracts bailing them out of major losses they had suffered in recent years (caused in large part by domestic asbestos and silica lawsuit settlements).

Senate Republicans have repeatedly blocked investigation attempts into the Halliburton/KBR contracts, the latest being S. Amdt. 2476 to S. 1042, which failed on a party-line vote (every Republican opposed, every Democrat supported). Sen. Martinez voted against it—if you're a Floridian and you're concerned, call his office and ask for an explanation. I sent him an e-mail over 3 weeks ago, and I'm still waiting for a response.

A few more detainees got out of the compounds last week, but this time one of our quick reaction teams caught them in the surrounding town. While our guys were patrolling the town, they noticed the extensive damage caused by the 12/10 fire-fight—apparently it was considerably worse than expected. Though, according to the Department of Defense (and our command here) it still never happened.

As for an update on the detainee abuse situation: I don't know whether my letter opened some new awareness in our leadership or whether they are just afraid that failure to change the environment here will lead to me addressing another letter a few levels higher in the chain-of-command (or to congress), but things here are a lot better. Just yesterday, I heard a soldier complaining that the TIF Commander told them that they are no longer allowed to use their iso-boxes. The iso-boxes here are about 20 ft. wide by 3 ft. deep by 4 ft. high. When detainees refused to cooperate, they would cram as many of them as would fit into those boxes for a few hours. Iso-boxes (of varying sizes) are used in just about every U.S. Army detention facility around the world. Our iso-boxes were one of the border-line items that I didn't include in my letter (I only listed clear and obvious deficiencies). But our leadership here now all-of-a-sudden feels that they are inhumane and are constructing new boxes that are of a more appropriate size; I'm very glad to see them take the initiative. I have had no more threats of reprisal, that conversation with my First Sergeant is actually the only time anybody has addressed this issue with me personally.

We've been assigned a third person to work at the office. SPC Strodtman (who we call by his nickname "Doughboy") is 22 years old and originally from Missouri. He isn't very experienced with computers or networking, but he's eager to learn and he's not afraid to get his hands dirty. Having him in the office has been a big help; its allowing me a couple hours a day of free time to unwind by reading, watching a movie, or playing video games.

Hope everything is going well back home. Talk to you later.
Mike

02/07/2006
Pictures—Week 10

I attached some pictures of my room. It's on the second floor and is 8 ft. x 10 ft. It's part of a bigger 24 ft. x 14 ft. cell that has been divided into 3 rooms by plywood. I'm lucky in that my room came furnished with a plywood desk and shelves (made by the Army carpenters here). Doughboy moved into the room right next to mine. Since we are only separated by a thin piece of plywood, there isn't much noise privacy—and unfortunately Doughboy is a big snorer.

During the Saddam days, it was one of the mass-holding cells. They would pack in as many inmates as possible, forcing them to literally live shoulder-to-shoulder with one another. The guards would periodically hand some food/water through the bars in the front of the cell (which can be seen in one of my pics)—and it would be passed around among the inmates. As you can imagine, the food would rarely make it all the way to the back of the cell—causing inmates who had been shoved to the back to starve to death.

When an inmate died, their body would be passed to the front by the other inmates, and the guards would remove the dead body and replace it with another prisoner. Life in the front of the cell (where my room is located) didn't always have its advantages—if inmates didn't starve to death at a quick enough rate to make room for the new prisoners, guards would open the door, indiscriminately shoot a dozen rounds into the cell, take out the bodies of whomever they killed (which were usually the guys in the front), and bring in the new prisoners.

I haven't seen any ghosts yet, but my room seems like it would be a good place to find them.

02/14/2006
Iraq Update—Week 11

Another week down. Not much is new here, so I'll pass along some answers to questions that I've been asked.

Let me preface by saying that I don't claim to be an expert on Iraq or the Middle East. I've just done some listening, and might be able to offer a slightly different perspective.

I've been asked whether the Iraqi Army has the capacity to handle the insurgency when we leave. I think that yes, they absolutely do—they handled it (under Saddam Hussein) before we arrived. The only difference is what constitutes an acceptable level of violence (on both sides).

The old standard was to ensure that the insurgency did not have the ability to topple the government—we have already achieved that, the insurgency is relegated to planting IEDs and firing a few rounds/mortars then running away; they don't have the capacity to launch an armed offensive.

The new standard seems to be total peace (no IEDs, no attacks, etc.). And while that's a worthy goal, this country has had insurgency for centuries (they were in the midst of a civil war when we invaded), and the hostility isn't all going to be wiped away in a matter of months, or years, or probably even decades.

The solution for "total peace" isn't really even a military one—it's a matter of creating an environment of trust and prosperity: establishing quality education and health care, equal access to government, entrepreneurial opportunities for everyone, etc.—things we are still working on in our own country.

It seems to me that the most important role that the Iraqi Army has in this process is border security—stop foreign terrorists (i.e., Zarqawi and his al-Qaeda cell) from coming into the country and killing people. It seems that the terrorist's indiscriminate killing of Arabs (using suicide bombers to blow up weddings/funerals/graduations/etc.) has finally caused them to wear out their welcome here; now even the Sunni insurgents are actively battling/killing them on the streets of Iraq. I think this statement from Sheikh Osama al-Jadaan, a local (and very influential) Sunni tribal leader, sums it up well: "We realized that these foreign terrorists were hiding behind the veil of the noble Iraqi resistance. They claim to be striking at the U.S. occupation, but the reality is they are killing innocent Iraqis in the markets, in mosques, in churches, and in our schools."

Border control is not rocket science, it's simply a matter of will and manpower (both of which the Iraqis have), so I'm confident that they can be successful in that endeavor. Though America may not be the best educators on how to secure a desert border, we are having trouble doing it ourselves with Mexico (we seem to lack the will).

I've heard speculation that when we leave, Iraq will collude with Iran in an anti-Western alliance. To me, this seems to fly in the face of thousands of years of history. While it is true that both Iraq and Iran will be governed by people who adhere to the Shi'ite sect of Islam, they have a different ethnicity: Iraqi Shi'ites are Arab, Iranian Shi'ites are Persian. They speak different languages and have different cultures. One thing which basically all Arabs (whether Shi'ite or Sunni) agree is that they don't trust Persians. The reasons for this date back over a millennia, but one of the more recent events is the Iran-Iraq War (1980–1988).

During the Iran-Iraq War (which lasted 8 years), Iraq suffered 1,000,000 casualties. To put this in perspective, if you add up all of the combat related deaths that the U.S. has suffered from EVERY war since our independence (230 years), it totals up to roughly the same number. Practically every Iraqi family (Shi'ite and Sunni) lost a father, son, or brother in that war—and of all Shi'ites I've spoken to, everyone I've asked have felt that Iraq was justified in waging that war. Saddam Hussein was very in tune with the prejudices of his people; he knew that a war against the Persians would unite the Iraqi people (both Sunni and Shi'ite) behind him.

The recently passed Iraqi Constitution states: "Arab people in Iraq are an inseparable part of the Arab nation"—nowhere does it mention any importance of being Shi'ite. I don't see any evidence that points to the proud "Arab nation" of Iraq all of a sudden submitting to become a puppet to the Persian nation of Iran.

I wouldn't lend too much credence to the Western media's portrayal of certain Iraqi political leaders as "pro-Iranian." During the Saddam days, those who voiced opposition to his atrocities would be incarcerated at Abu Ghraib (many times along with members of their family) and very often be executed. This caused most political dissidents to acquiesce and live a life of fearful silence, some had the courage to leave their possessions behind and flee to neighboring Iran and from there dedicate their lives to the overthrow of Saddam Hussein. The Western media has taken a liking to referring to those in the latter category as "pro-Iranian"—but their residence in Iran was in opposition to Saddam, not in support of Tehran. It is not surprising to me that those who had risked their lives to remain in the region and work to bring about a democratic Iraq would be among Iraq's first elected leaders; I don't see anything in their ideology or political positions that in any way indicates solidarity with Iran.

I've also been asked whether I think that the average Iraqi citizen is capable of performing their civic duty in a democracy. Well, from my perspective, in some ways they are more capable than the average American. I've found them generally to be more involved (less apathetic) and more passionate in their beliefs; lets not forget they had a 75%-plus voter turnout rate, when they were literally risking their lives and walking through miles of desert to do so. In America we can barely scrape above 40% with P. Diddy and commercials begging people to please drive their cars by the poll on their way to work—and if the line to vote is longer than 30 minutes many Americans will abandon the process in a huff (which I've personally witnessed). So yes, I think they are capable. Not to sound condescending, but I'm actually very proud of them.

I don't know how well-publicized this was back home, but about 2 weeks ago the Sunnis offered a deal to end the insurgency and join the political process in full. Some of the stipulations were: a halt to random arrests (any arrest without a court order), the resignation of the current Iraqi Interior Minister (who they deem is responsible for the execution of numerous Sunni prisoners), an apology from the U.S. and Iraqi govt. for detainees who have died while being held without charges, that the Iraqi police be replaced by the Iraqi army in regions where police brutality against Sunni prisoners is prevalent, and that the results of investigations into secret Iraqi prisons (which were discovered by U.S. troops) be released.

Virtually all of the demands in some way relate to detainee abuse, making it very clear that the reason this insurgency still exists at its current level is because of our inability to adhere to basic human rights standards (like the Geneva Convention) and demand the same from our Iraqi allies. So for those who may think that detainee abuse is necessary to intimidate or acquire information to effectively battle the insurgency, it appears there wouldn't even be much of an insurgency left to battle if the abuse hadn't been committed in the first place. The U.S. and Iraqi governments have yet to give a formal response to the offer.

Hope all is well. Talk to you later.
Mike

02/14/2006
Pictures—Week 11

Since not all of the detainees here can read, the rules they are required to follow have been printed in a cartoon type picture form on a big canvas banner. These banners are posted in the compounds. I find some of the cartoons to be amusing. I attached two pictures of different areas of the banner.

I also attached a picture of the hookah pipe that I purchased a few weeks back. Hookah pipes are a fundamental part of the Arab culture. The hookah is used to smoke shisha, which is tobacco leaf mixed with molasses and dried fruit. A wide variety of flavors are available (so far, I've tried apple, strawberry, orange, and mixed fruit). The smoke really does smell quite good—like a flavored potpourri. Personally, I still prefer a good cigar (and thanks to some generous care packages, I have a good supply), but the hookah provides a nice and interesting change of pace.

أطع كافة قوانين المعسكر
لاتستهن بالآخرين
على المعتقلين إطاعة وإحترام
كافة الحراس والمنتسبين

ممنوع تهديد المعتقلين الآخرين
ممنوع إقامة علاقات
جنسية مع المعتقلين
ممنوع البصاق

FINE POINT
PERMANENT MARKER

02/20/2006
Iraq Update—Week 12

I've been asked what are the best and worst aspects of being deployed to Iraq.

The two best things about being deployed to Iraq:

1. The pecan pie.
2. ?????

The pecan pie is pretty good, and when they have it (which is not very often), I can get as much as I want. They don't make it here; it's actually shipped into the country. I really can't think of a second item—sorry, I tried.

The two worst things about being deployed to Iraq:

1. Being separated from the people I care about.
2. The static environment.

The first one is self-explanatory, and is by far the worse of the two. As for the environment, it's not so much that there are limited luxuries—the worst part is that day in and day out I am stuck in the same dreary surroundings. Actually, I think that if you locked somebody up in Disney World's Magic Kingdom, for the first week or so they may enjoy themselves, but as the months roll by they're going to get stir-crazy and start wanting to break down the gate. Freedom of movement seems to be an innate human desire.

However, life here is still considerably better than the FOB at Ft. Dix. Here are five reasons why:

1. My job (and living quarters) gives me a certain level of independence.
2. I have plenty of Internet access.
3. I have a single room with heat and a/c (instead of sharing a tent with 11 other guys).
4. The microwave and packages you guys send allow me to eat some normal food.
5. Warm daily showers.

I also no longer have to listen to guys who have never been in a combat-zone try to explain one to me (most of what they said was wrong).

I've been asked about some of my friends in my unit. Unfortunately, I hardly ever see people in my company (652 MP) anymore, they all live and work on the other side of the post. But being separated from them does have its advantages—it means that I really don't have any chain-of-command around to "supervise" me. The rest of the guys in my unit have to concern themselves with a variety of arbitrary rules and polices, such as weekly in-room inspections—like the soldiers here don't have enough on their mind without having to worry about whether their socks and underwear are folded in the correct manner.

We've been getting shelled semi-regularly (a few times a week) for the past month—sometimes they hit close to me, other times they hit a different area of the post. When we are attacked, everyone goes to their company's Tactical Operation Center (TOC), so that an accurate headcount can be taken (to assess casualties), and they remain there until the "all clear" is given. Since my company (and our TOC) is about a half a mile away (in a different LSA), it would be impractical for me to traverse that distance under enemy fire—so they know not to expect me. I usually respond by putting on my body armor and Kevlar helmet and going into the hallway to assess the situation and find out what our response is going to be so that I'm readily available if vehicles roll out to defend the post.

So far, our response to mortar attacks has just been to return fire with artillery of our own. They fire in a medium size mortar, we shoot out some large mortars, they fire in another medium size mortar, we shoot out more large mortars, etc. It's kind of like a big deadly pissing contest. So I usually end up just going back to the office (or my room) and continuing whatever it is I was doing—I figure it's just as likely for me to be blown up while I'm on my laptop in my office or in my room as it is while I'm standing around in a hallway or TOC. Last week I was on Instant Messenger with Kendra during a mortar attack. I'm sure that chatting on the Internet and being on the webcam in the midst of an enemy attack is something that is new and unique to this war.

At the barber shop, a shoulder massage is included with the price of a haircut ($3)—it must be some sort of cultural practice. A few weeks ago, I noticed that the lights were off in that building, but I was in need of a haircut so I ventured over to see if they were open, and sure enough, the door was unlocked. As I walked through the door I saw that the room, while usually crowded, contained only two people: the Iraqi barber and a soldier from my unit. Even more unusual, the room was aglow in candlelight, soft music was playing in the background, and the soldier had his head leaned back while the barber gently worked his hands across the young man's shoulders.

The soldier must have realized how the situation would be perceived, because upon seeing me enter the room, he straightened up in his chair and hurriedly shouted: "Sergeant, the powers out! I really needed a haircut, so we used the candles so he could see!" I just shook my head and let out a little chuckle. The barber then followed up with "I'm almost done with him. If you wait, I can do you next." His choice of words caused the soldier to look even more mortified. I just replied with a "No thanks" and walked out the door. While I don't think there was any "don't ask, don't tell" activity occurring, I figured it would be best for all parties if I left them to their privacy. I'm actually the only person whom I know that opts out of the massage; I haven't been here long enough to find the prospects of some Iraqi guy rubbing on me to be appealing.

I saw that more photos of the 2003 Abu Ghraib atrocities were publicized this week. This provides us with an excellent opportunity to reflect on SPC Joseph Darby, the reservist who worked on the military computer network here, and who after stumbling across those pictures, pushed them up his chain-of-command (which ultimately lead to the brutality being publicized). He returned from Iraq to have his home vandalized and be inundated with chants of "Rat" and "Traitor." He and his family are still living in protective custody at an undisclosed location because of the continued threats against their lives.

I depart for my two-week leave in a couple of days. I'm very excited that I get to return home to see how much Morgan has grown, to spend some time with Kendra, and get a brief taste of normalcy; it will be my first time home in nearly 6 months. I get 14 full days at home, so with the travel time, I'll be away from Abu for about 3 weeks. My e-mail updates will resume upon my return back here.

Hope all is well. Talk to you later. See many of you soon!
Mike

02/20/2006
Pictures—Week 12

I attached a picture of the Iraqi sky; it's a view over the compounds. The palm trees are off post, on the other side of the outer walls.

03/21/2006
Iraq Update—Week 30

Well, I'm back here at Abu Ghraib. My leave went really well—it was actually two of the best weeks of my life. It's difficult for me to express just how much I enjoy spending time with Kendra and Morgan. They are two really amazing people; I'm very fortunate to have them in my life.

At first, being at home felt kind of surreal. On Thursday (2/23) I was at Abu surrounded by people literally trying to kill me, then by Monday (2/27) I was surrounded by small children with Morgan on my lap singing along with a frog puppet. But by the end of my second day home I had fallen back into the old groove, with Iraq fading into the back of my mind like a three day old nightmare.

Morgan has certainly grown a lot. The last time I saw her she was still pretty much a baby, now she's so much a little girl: playing tea with her dolls, dancing, communicating, etc. It's really an awesome thing to see. I wish that I could be more a part of it.

When I enlisted four and a half years ago, I knew that I was making a sacrifice. But at the time, Morgan wasn't even a glimmer in my eye. The time that I am now missing with her is priceless; it's worth more to me than anything else in the world, and there is no way to regain the moments that I've missed.

I also thought that I was doing something selfless; I've come to realize that my decision has forced a burden on many others: from the people whom I work with, to my parents, and of course, Kendra; her sacrifices may be even greater than my own. Had I known that my decision would have this great of an impact on the lives of others, I may have gathered their input instead of just treating it as a personal decision and imposing this obligation on everyone. I really hope that all of our efforts end up being worth something, that the Iraqis don't squander the opportunity for liberty that we've given them.

My two weeks went by way too fast, and before I knew it I was at the airport headed back to Iraq. Having to turn away from my little girl waving goodbye in my wife's arms and walk onto the airplane was the hardest thing that I've ever had to do—it's the only time in my life that I've felt completely broken.

People have a tendency of trying to divide the world into distinct opposites: good/evil, night/day, beautiful/ugly, joy/pain, etc. In reality, one can only be understood in relation to the other. For example, we could not comprehend the idea of "night" without also having the concept of "day;" the one is only realized because of the existence of the other. In the same way, we would not have an awareness of joy, without also feeling pain. I'm trying to hold on to this thought as I sit here really missing my wife and daughter—without this pain that I'm currently feeling, there wouldn't be an appreciation for the great joy of our eventual reunification and the time we spend together then after. But it's hard.

A lot of soldiers come back from leave feeling rejuvenated; all I feel is an overwhelming sense of despair.

You might have noticed that my week count in the subject line of the e-mail jumped from 12 to 30. Since I left Iraq and came back, I really didn't want to start back at one. So I'm now counting from the date I was activated, which will remain unchanged. Hopefully I will be home before it reaches 65—which is the day before Thanksgiving.

Hope all is well. Talk to you later.
Mike

03/28/2006
Iraq Update—Week 31

I'm starting to get back into my old routine. As expected, nothing had changed here during my time away.

While I was home, one thing that I really appreciated was how supportive everyone was—not just family and friends, but also complete strangers. At the airport on my way back here, I had two different people buy me lunch, and an employee at Starbucks gave me a free cup of coffee (even the little things mean a lot).

After saying goodbye to Kendra and Morgan and heading into the terminal, there was an elderly couple in front of me in line to board our airplane, both of whom were on the verge of tears. We were at the end of the line, and I guess some of the people in front of us were taking their time settling into their seats, so we stood there in place for quite a while. I wondered what it was that had them so upset, but I figured it would be rude to ask. As the minutes went by, I noticed that they would look at me and then look away quickly, not wanting to make eye contact.

Eventually as the line started to move again, the woman turned back and asked me where I was headed; I confirmed what I'm sure they had already expected, that I was on my way back to Iraq. She replied that they both really appreciated what I was doing. Then her husband, still looking off in the distance, softly said "I was in Korea". I then realized that it must have been the sight of me saying goodbye to my wife and daughter that had put them in their saddened condition, possibly invoking memories of their own painful goodbye decades earlier.

I could tell that he was having difficulty searching for the words to tell me something. He then pulled a small folded-up plastic bag out of his pocket, and from it removed a little lapel pin. He said: "I got this at the Football Hall of Fame in Canton, Ohio. I want you to have it." It seemed an odd thing for him to give me, but I thanked him, and he continued: "When you come home, you should check it out if you're ever up that way. It's really nice there." They wished me luck, and we parted ways to our respective seats.

It wasn't until I arrived at my seat that I realized that what he had given me was more than just a little trinket; he had given me a physical reminder that my departure is only temporary, that one day in the not too distant future I'll be back home—and maybe even vacationing in Ohio. This little NFL Hall of Fame pin means more to me than all of the medals and ribbons that the Army has awarded me. I keep it on the shelf above my bed.

As far as my morale is concerned, I guess it's about as good as can be expected. Though I am finding it increasingly difficult to feel concern for the Iraqi people and their problems when I have my own people and my own issues back home which are considerably more important to me. It was easier to be here when I actually cared.

Before we left New Jersey, the teenage soldiers in my unit were pulled aside and told that going to war would turn boys into men. I'm not so sure about that—but in my case, it seems to have turned a man into an old man; these 4 months in Iraq feel like they've aged me 10 years: my back is stiff, I have hemorrhoids, and my idealism is disintegrating.

Hope all is well. Talk to you later.
Mike

04/04/2006
Iraq Update—Week 32

Well, another week down. I've managed to drag myself out of self-pity mode. There are more important things in this world than my own personal happiness; I think we all probably need to be reminded of that every once in a while.

When I was back home, I was often asked about the term "unit": "What do you mean by your unit?", "How many people are in a unit?" etc.

While OPSEC (operational security) prohibits me from giving precise details on the composition of my specific unit, I can answer the broader question of what a unit is, how mine originated, and very generally what we are doing here.

When a soldier refers to their "unit," what they're usually alluding to is their "company" (called a "battery" for those in artillery). A company/battery can have anywhere from 70 to 200 soldiers, with the precise number being determined by what it is that they do (i.e., infantry companies require more soldiers than armor companies). However, the typical company is between 120 to 180 soldiers.

Prior to our activation in August, my unit (the 652nd MP Company) did not exist; we were formed specifically for this mission and will be disbanded immediately upon our redeployment home. To form the nucleus of this new Military Police company, one entire artillery battery was activated. I was a member of that battery, as is virtually all of the leadership in the 652 MP CO.

Since there were significantly fewer soldiers in the artillery battery than necessary to properly staff an MP company (as is the nature of their differing functions), soldiers were plucked from various other companies from around the state to fill in gaps. So even though we are called an "MP company," there is nobody in my unit actually trained (MOS qualified) as an MP; we are a hodge-podge of artillerymen, air-defenders, mechanics, clerks, etc.

The first time we all got together as the 652nd MP CO was at the initial mobilization, about two weeks before we hopped on a plane for Ft. Dix. Prior to that about half of the unit (those in the old artillery battery) had never met the other half, and some soldiers (those plucked out of units by themselves) had never met ANYONE in the new company. So to a large extent, we arrived in New Jersey as strangers.

Our time at Ft. Dix was stressful, the environment was pretty grueling, and a lot of people really didn't get along with one another. But our 10 weeks of training went a long way in bonding us all together into a fairly cohesive team. Unfortunately, it did an extremely poor job in training us for the actual mission that we were assigned here in Iraq.

Out of about 70 days of training, only 5 were set aside for instruction on detainee operations; and in those 5 days, not a single piece of relevant information was disseminated. The first day was spent spraying us in the eyes with pepper spray. On the second day we learned how to fill out paperwork (which isn't even applicable to our mission here). The third and fourth days were spent learning outdated riot control techniques designed for handling mass open-field riots (like 1960s U.S. Vietnam War protests) that in no way resemble what guards deal with here (the environment, the tools, and the methods are completely different). And the fifth day was spent entirely on "forced-cell extraction" techniques which I don't think are used anywhere outside of U.S. prisons—certainly not in detainee compounds where cells don't even exist.

Some of the soldiers in my unit are right out of high school, others worked in the mall or grocery store, we have a few who had just started college. Here at Abu Ghraib, about 90–95% of them are working as guards in the compounds. They have absolutely zero relevant training and no similar life experiences to draw upon in their new jobs—it is a recipe for absolute disaster (apparently the Army learned nothing from their past mistakes here).

Their work is completely thankless. The detainees hate them, the active-duty soldiers look down on them, the world is suspect of them. They work close to 14-hour days; and for the few conscious hours when they aren't on duty, there is really nothing here on post to help them escape from the intense, physically and emotionally draining daily grind (my Internet service is pretty much it).

I've seen a lot of what U.S. troops are doing over here, and without a doubt their job is the most difficult there is in Iraq; making it quite possibly the most difficult job in the world. Their days are much tougher than mine.

And despite all that, despite the odds stacked against them, the young men and women in my unit have done an extraordinary job. "Extraordinary" doesn't even do it justice. I don't think there is an adjective capable of describing just how impressed I am by their performance. They are professionals in every respect of the word.

You should all be very proud to be citizens of a nation who produces such young people as these—I know I am. So, the next time I'm feeling depressed or lacking in motivation, I need look no further than the soldiers serving beside me for inspiration.

Hope all is well back home. Talk to you later.
Mike

04/11/2006
Iraq Update—Week 33

I thought I should include some clarification between what may be perceived as discrepancies between statements made in my last e-mail and those made in e-mails prior. Every failing in the administration of this facility that I have mentioned in the past have been the responsibility of those in higher echelons of the chain of command; officers and civilians who have had the training, the access to the information, and the power necessary to correct the problems. The enlisted soldiers in my unit do not have the ability to control those individuals or the policies that they impose; that I have, is a result of life experiences granting me a different set of tools to work with. The young men and women whom I praised last week have served admirably, with discipline and honor; they have served to the best of their abilities, and have surpassed even my high expectations. As stated last week, I am very proud to serve with them.

Yesterday at breakfast chow, I sat at a table with a Specialist and a Warrant Officer. We were making small talk, discussing our assignments, and the conversation eventually turned to enemy engagement. The Specialist said: "Man, I'm hoping for a Purple Heart. Nothing serious, maybe just some shrapnel in the leg or something." The Warrant Officer chimed in: "What I really want is a CAB (combat action badge), just some exterior damage to my Humvee, nothing where I get hurt or anything." Then they both looked at me. I just sat there for a second, trying to comprehend the mindset of one who hopes for potential death in return for a little piece of metal or a cloth patch, and I replied: "Hell, all I want is my DD-214 (honorable discharge from active duty). I'll leave the glory to you guys; I'm just trying to get out of here with all of my limbs intact." The two soldiers looked at each other, a few moments passed, and I think my point set in. The Warrant Officer ended the conversation with: "I think the Sergeant here is the only smart one at the table."

I have a tremendous amount of respect for those who have earned medals of valor, but I have no desire to be thrust into the position required to achieve one, especially if it's simply for the purpose of acquiring that recognition. I have long passed the point in my life where I seek the validation or the approval of others, I don't feel the need to be anyone's "hero."

I remember at Ft. Dix sitting next to a soldier on a sandbag as we caught our breath for a few moments in-between training missions. I could tell there was something weighing heavy on his mind, so I nudged him on the leg and asked him how everything was going. He continued to stare at the ground, but said:

"You know, I guess if we have to die, going out in a war is probably the best way to go." I replied "Hey," and he looked up at me as I continued: "if we get a choice, then I choose to die of old age, for the both of us."

Insurgent activity is on the rise here at Abu Ghraib—we had another young man killed in action this week, and several other serious casualties in separate attacks. Hopefully things will improve here someday.

Hope all is well back home. Talk to you later.
Mike

04/18/2006
Iraq Update—Week 34

Here are questions that I am continually asked: "Is it really as bad as the media says it is over there? Is the news coverage fair and accurate?" They are difficult questions to answer. While I try to keep my finger on the pulse of the overall situation by talking with as many people as possible, all I can really speak to with any certainty are the things that I personally experience.

To answer the questions, the first thing that needs to determined is: what exactly makes something newsworthy? Generally, I think that a particular story requires some deviation from the norm. For example, if a guy gets into his car, drives to the post-office, and comes home, it's not going to be on the nightly news because similar situations occur thousands of times every day. However, if the guy drives to the post-office and shoots up everybody inside, now that's a page one story. As the old news axiom goes: "If it bleeds, it leads."

There isn't anything necessarily wrong with that. Personally, I wouldn't read a paper whose articles were simply a series of stories like: "John Smith went to the post-office today, stood in line, and went home." Getting the deviation is important, but it's also important for the consumer to keep in mind the overall context (the environment) in which it's occurring—just because a post-office shooting is in the news, it doesn't mean that they are common-place, and it isn't a good reflection of the overall security or risk of visiting one.

I was here at Abu the day the Al-Askari Mosque (a.k.a., "The Golden Dome") was bombed in Samarra; and the morning after, I was on a convoy through western Baghdad. When I arrived at my destination, I had a few hours to kill, so I went to a lounge and turned on CNN. What I saw was the anchorman and all of the pundits declaring that a "civil war" had broken out in Iraq—that there was violence, rioting, and pandemonium in the streets. Their statements did not match the situation that I personally saw on the ground. In the area through which I had just convoyed, there was absolutely no difference between that morning and any other morning: farmers were out tending to their fields, women were hanging their laundry, children were playing with the sheep and asking us for candy, there was not a single hint of unrest—and this was IN Baghdad.

Now, I'm sure that the news was not entirely false, I don't think that they doctored the video footage, I'm sure that violence had broken out in PARTS of Iraq—but that seemed to be the deviation from the norm. All of the Iraqis that I saw were proceeding with their daily lives as usual; and in fact, later reports showed that in 14 of the 18 Iraqi provinces there was virtually no violence.

Don't get me wrong, I'm not trying to say that Iraq is any more or less dangerous or fragile than is being portrayed in the news. Honestly, I really don't know one way or the other (I cannot accurately make sweeping statements about the entire nation)—to reiterate, all I can really speak for is what I personally experience. But, the same is also true for the media; and the dirty little secret that they don't tell you is that they are pretty much relegated to an area known as "the green zone"—which is a highly fortified part of Baghdad. The vast majority of reporters in Iraq have probably never even heard a gun fired in anger.

While this is by their choice, it's not entirely their fault. There have been something like 80 reporters killed since the war began, and I don't blame them for not wanting to add to that statistic. But, the news outlets should be a little more candid when the anchorman goes to the "In Baghdad" reporter to validate their comments by making it clear that the reporter is relying on third-and fourth-hand information, and is really not in any better position to comment on the situation than a reporter sitting in Washington DC. They are not eye-witnesses; when they claim there is violence in the streets, they are merely speculating or regurgitating something somebody else told them. All of the real "embedded" reporters seem to have either been killed or gone home.

Which creates a problem, if those who are here in Iraq don't have the capacity to discern the overall context in which a newsworthy event is occurring, how can the consumer at home possibly do it?

Of course, the fact that reporters are afraid to leave their protected area to actually go do real reporting is probably a pretty good indication of the overall security situation. Here at Abu Ghraib, things definitely aren't any better then when I first arrived (we had three more guys killed this week). That's really the best answer I can give you.

One thing that I find interesting is that being over here I get the opportunity to view the U.S. from the outside looking in. Here is a sampling of the news headlines from the past week:

* Millions pack streets to protest immigration bill;
* U.S. President plans to use nuclear weapons against Iran;
* Gulf Coast still a "disaster area" as new hurricane season approaches;
* Americans agree: Congress is corrupt;
* Chicago sting nets 150 murderers, rapists, and child abductors;
* Escalating gang violence put schools on edge;
* Suspect identified in execution-style massacre in Seattle;
* Bomb blast destroys church bus in Minnesota;

Now I ask all of you: Is the news coverage fair and accurate? Is it really as bad as the media says it is over there? The answer probably depends in large part as to whether you are a Mexican immigrant, resident of New Orleans, or a white guy in Tampa.

Hope all is well. Talk to you later.
Mike

04/25/2006
Iraq Update—Week 35

For those of you who don't know, I was moved to the compounds this week. While I'm disappointed that I'll no longer be working in a job that I don't detest, I understand the necessity of the move.

The first line of the "Warrior Ethos" goes: "I will always place the mission first." The mission that my unit, the 652nd MP Company, has been assigned by CENTCOM is detainee operations at Abu Ghraib; and with soldiers scheduled to go on leave in the coming months, there was set to be a shortage of guards in the compounds. So while it's clear that the Internet here is critical to the morale of the soldiers, the morale of the soldiers is not the priority of the Army, or my unit especially. I will also be changing rooms, moving over to my company's area, sometime in the next week or so.

I began my new job on Thursday at 13:00. I was assigned to the level responsible for guarding all of the juveniles and all of the detainees who practice the Shia form of Islam.

I will really miss having all of that access to the Internet, with the ability to talk to Kendra via Yahoo Instant Messenger every day.

I'll also miss working with SGT Ballou. It really was refreshing to work with somebody so knowledgeable in their field. We've become pretty good friends; I feel bad that he is now stuck with Doughboy by himself.

After about two weeks in the office, Doughboy pretty much gave up on trying to get a grasp of the system; and instead just spends his time sitting in the corner talking to his wife on the computer and playing video games (for the few hours that he even shows up).

Actually, his tendency of making ridiculous comments created additional problems for us. One example was his explanation to a Captain of our room installation policy. Ballou and my policy was that installs are done on a first-come, first-served basis. So if a Private comes in on Monday and requests an install, then a Colonel comes in on Tuesday and requests one; the Private is going to get hooked-up first (and vice-versa)—when it comes to communication with your family back home, rank is not an issue.

Well, for some incomprehensible reason, Doughboy told a Captain that the policy is: "enlisted soldiers are hooked-up first, and officers go at the end of the list"—of course, that angered the officer, and he complained of discrimination to our higher-ups, requiring Ballou and myself to go through a painstaking effort to correct the record. It really isn't Doughboy's fault, he's just not suited for anything cerebral.

Since Doughboy does not have the capacity to manage the network, when Ballou's unit leaves for Cropper (and his unit is the first scheduled to go) the Internet here will be completely shut down—unless of course, the higher-ups decide to move me back to my old position prior to that time.

Hope all is well. Talk to you later.
Mike

05/02/2006
Iraq Update—Week 36

I guess some of you are wondering why (with my knowledge) they didn't move Doughboy from the Internet office instead of moving me. Well, there was really no reasoning, logic, or common-sense behind that decision—it was simply the result of petty company politics. But, there is no point in dwelling on things that are out of my control, so on to life working in the compounds.

The detainee compounds are entirely outdoors, and a gravel road runs down the center of the level. The gravel is of the typical type that would be used to make a parking lot, or that you may find in a construction zone—the only noticeable difference being that the color has been completely washed away from seasons of oppressive sunlight. Only two vehicles use the road: the truck used to clean the porta-johns, and a Humvee used to deliver food and pick up trash.

The road in my level has been named "Dirka-Dirka Blvd" (which may be amusing to those of you who have seen *Team America: World Police*), and it divides two columns of tents, with every tent facing the road.

Each tent is surrounded by a chain link fence that is covered in concertina wire. Each fenced-in tent houses about 30 detainees, and has a single gate, which is locked with a padlock.

To the right of each tent's gate, sitting just outside of the fence, there is a plywood box with a plexiglass front, which contains a 32" TV, DVD player, and radio for the detainee's amusement.

There is a red drum located inside the fence, in the front left corner of every tent area. The detainees are permitted to fill up the drum with water twice a day (once every shift). The drum is elevated over a small pit which collects the falling water (giving the detainees a place to wash their jumpsuits). Within the fence, each tent also has a blue porta-john and a small concrete bunker (so that cover is available when we get shelled).

There is no concrete flooring in the compounds, with the exception of the gravel road, the ground is completely dirt. Small irrigation trenches have been dug along the back of each tent to provide drainage for when it rains.

A guard tower, located in the middle of the southern most perimeter, looms over the level. It is really nothing more than rusted orange shipping containers, stacked one upon another, with a wooden guard shack placed on top, and a scaffolding staircase pushed up to one side.

A small sliver of shadow cast from "The Tower" peeks over the southern most portion of the level for a few moments out of the day; this the only shade ever present in the compound. A detainee must go inside their tent to escape the direct rays of the sun; for the soldiers, there is a small guard shack present in each of the four "zones" on the level—but 90% of our time is spent directly in the sun (and the temperature is already over 100 degrees). We are required to wear our helmet and full body armor for the entire 13 hour shift.

The guard shacks are roughly 6 ft. x 6 ft., constructed entirely of plywood and plexiglass, and surrounded by two 4-ft. stacks of green sandbags.

There are power-generated light posts situated in between each tent and surrounding the perimeter of the level that we turn on at night to illuminate the area.

A pungent odor permeates the facility; and flies, mosquitoes, beetles, and various other strange Middle Eastern insects are ever-present. This is where I have worked for the past two weeks, and will continue to spend 12 hours of every day for the next 6 months.

The entire level is surrounded by more chain link fence and concertina wire. Just inside the perimeter fencing, to the left of the main gate, sits a 4 ft. wide x 6 ft. long x 7 ft. high cell, with both horizontal and vertical bars, made entirely of steel. This is the SEG Box; it is used as both a holding area for detainees waiting to be picked up for appointments, and detainees can be placed there for a few hours as punishment for failing to follow our instructions.

The Control Point is located just outside of the perimeter fence; it is a small wooden structure, furnished with a couple of desks and computers hooked-up to the military computer network.

Hope all is well back home. Talk to you later.
Mike

05/09/2006
Iraq Update—Week 37

Well, another week down. I've now settled into the routine of working in the compounds. There are a couple of different jobs that I rotate through throughout the week.

Some days I'm assigned to be a Rover. The basic function of this position is to constantly patrol the yard, ensuring that the facility is secure, and that detainees are adhering to the camp rules. The rules that the detainees are required to follow are pretty simple: no screaming across the wire to detainees in other tents, they must wear their jump-suit pants, and follow our instructions.

A rover is also required to escort detainees to/from the sally-port and main-gate when they enter and exit the facility; and they rotate into the tower for 3 to 5 hours out of the day to provide over-watch for the yard.

Some days I'm assigned to be a Zone Rep. The main responsibility of this position is detainee accountability; they must be aware of location and have precise counts of all the detainees in their zone. Detainees are constantly coming and going throughout the day (to school, family visitation, the hospital, court, interrogations, etc.). So Zone Reps are always busy updating their numbers. They also maintain possession of the keys to the gates for the tents in their zone; so their presence is required any time one of their detainees enters or exists the yard; and they are responsible for all of the soldier weapons/inventory for their zone.

The Zone Rep handles the vast majority of the detainee interaction. They are responsible for handing out supplies, taking requests/complaints, performing tadots (headcounts), calling wahed-wahed (making the detainees get in the tent for sleep or lockdown), turning on/off the radio, and playing the DVDs for each tent in their zone. They personally handle minor detainee requests (if they get extra water/supplies, hair clippers that day, etc.).

With some of the leadership in my unit going on leave, I've also had the opportunity to be the Yard Dog a little sooner than expected. The area where all of the detainees live is called "the yard"—and the Yard Dog is responsible for everything that happens in that area. His main function is to supervise the Rovers and Zone Reps.

The Yard Dog is also given a daily list of appointments for all of the detainees, and ensures that they are in the SEG Box at the appropriate time to be transported. He confirms that all of the Zone Rep's detainee counts are correct, and he handles virtually all of the communication from the yard to the Control Point.

So basically, the Zone Reps report to the Yard Dog, and the Yard Dog reports to the Control Point.

The Yard Dog makes most of the operational decisions for the level (e.g., tent assignments, whether medics are called, tent visitations, etc.); because of the responsibility, he must be a Non-Commissioned Officer.

There is a computer operator inside of the Control Point who performs all of the data entry (into a system called DIMs) to annotate everything significant that happens inside of the yard. The Shift Leader is also posted in the Control Point. He is in-charge of soldier scheduling (who does what job), and communicates information from the Yard Dog to higher echelons.

I've heard from the Shift Leader that I may have an opportunity to rotate into the DIMs operator position sometime in the near future. Since that job is mostly indoors and has little physical contact with the detainees, I think that I would find it preferable to some of my current duties. I still haven't gotten used to the stench of body odor that exists throughout the yard.

So far, the weekly rotation has been that I work 2 days as a Zone Rep, 2 days as Yard Dog (on the regular Yard Dog and Shift Leaders days off), and 2 days as Rover.

I moved into my new room on Saturday, it's about 6 ft. x 8 ft. and has concrete walls and a steel door (so I wont be hearing the noises/snoring of my neighbors). Of course, it's over in my company's area, so now I have to be prepared for inspections and to follow all of their crazy little rules.

Hope all is well. Talk to you later.
Mike

05/16/2006
Iraq Update—Week 38

I figured that I'd use this e-mail to walk you through what a typical day is like for me here.

11:30 am—My alarm rings, I roll out of bed, put on my flip-flops, and walk over to the shower trailers to shave and brush my teeth; then I come back to my room and put on my uniform and boots.

12:15—I turn on my laptop and quickly get online to browse the news of the day for about 15 minutes.

12:30—I check my bag to ensure that all of my necessary equipment is present, I put on my helmet and body armor, and walk over to the motor pool.

12:45—I hop on a truck which delivers me and the other soldiers on my shift in my level to Guard Mount.

13:00—We line up in formation and are briefed by the Shift Leader as to what our assignment will be for the day (for this example I'll be the #2 Zone Rep), then every soldier on-shift from every level files into the chapel to receive the daily Military Intelligence (MI) Briefing. The MI Briefing is basically just an overview of what happened in the compounds over the last 11 hours (riots, fights, assaults on guards, etc.), and enemy activity in the surrounding area over the last 24 hours (small arms attacks, IEDs, mortars, etc.).

13:45—We get back in the truck and head over to our level to relieve the other shift and begin our day in the compounds.

As soon as we walk through the main gate the barrage begins: "Sergeant! Sergeant! Sergeant!" "I hungry," "Light cigarette," "I need visit Tent 14," "No water, need hose," "Throw me ball (because they knocked it over the fence)," etc. I must hear them scream the word "sergeant" over a thousand times a day—they are relentless.

14:00—I'll walk over to each tent in my zone and tell the detainee closest to the gate to assemble the other detainees for tadot (headcount). After I count the detainees and ensure that the correct number are present, I have them line up in Internee Serial Number (ISN) order so that I can check their ISNs to ensure that the individual detainees are in their proper locations. I'll then update the log book and the white board in my zone shack, and radio my numbers in to the Yard Dog.

Then I will go through all of the weapons in my Zone Shack (shotgun, lethal and non-lethal rounds, flashbangs, ball grenades, baton, OC foggers, flex-cuffs, etc.) to ensure that everything is in proper working condition.

When that is completed, I'll make the first rounds (of many throughout the day) to each tent to see if there is anything they need besides the usual cigarette light, ball fetching, etc. I'll usually have a couple of tents who want to use the rec yard to play soccer, and some will want 510s (request forms) to make a complaint or inquiry—which is pointless; none of the guards can ever remember seeing a request approved.

Usually around this time there will be a batch of detainees that need to be taken to school or an appointment (medical, radiology, MI, etc.). So, I'll pull them out, move them to the Seg Box, and update my log book and board.

16:00—A truck will arrive with the detainee's dinner chow. Their food is always the same: white rice, pita bread, chai tea, and chicken chunks in an orange broth (which kind of looks like tomato soup). There are six detainees assigned to the "chow detail" that divvies up the food into the appropriate portions for each tent; so I'll pull them out of their tent and supervise their work. Each tent has one container for their rice, one container for their chicken "soup," a box for their bread and tea, and the appropriate amount of plastic bottles and plates. When the chow detail has finished dividing the food and tea into the containers and boxes, I escort them as they deliver it to each tent.

16:30—A Rover and a Zone Rep are selected by the Yard Dog to go pick up chow for the other soldiers on shift in the level. They'll drive over to the DFAC, grab a few dozen Styrofoam boxes, go through the chow line to get them filled with food, and drive them back to the compounds. This process usually takes about an hour. We eat our food in the Zone Shacks.

Usually around this time we'll be receiving the detainees returning from their morning appointments (sent out by the other shift). So, I'll put them back in their tents, and update the log book and board.

19:30—I'll go back around to each tent and perform another tadot, verify that my numbers are correct, and radio them in to the Yard Dog. When that's done I'll turn off the radios for each tent, turn on their TVs and DVD players, and put in a movie for them to watch. For the next 4 and a half hours I will be harassed incessantly to change movies. Satisfying all of the detainees is impossible; one day I felt extra-accommodating and I changed a tent's DVD 7 times in 2 hours—it did nothing to reduce the complaining.

20:30—I'll pull the 6 detainee "trash detail" and escort them as they take the filled trash bags (and empty food containers) from the front of each tent to the dumpster. Two detainees from the "chow detail" will also be pulled to clean the containers.

22:00—I'll go back around to each tent and perform another tadot and another ISN check, verify my numbers are correct, and radio them in to the Yard Dog. When that's completed, the Yard Dog will tell us which tent has been selected for a "shakedown" that evening. We'll pull all of the detainees from that tent, pat them down, and move them into the rec yard, then begin rifling through everything in their tent (blankets, boxes, sleeping mats, etc.). This usually takes about an hour.

23:00—Another couple of soldiers are selected by the Yard Dog to go pick up chow for the soldiers.

24:00—I'll do another tadot, turn off the TVs, and call "wahed-wahed," which means that all of the detainees have to go into their tent. For the rest of the night only one detainee is allowed out of the tent at a time.

02:00—The other shift arrives to relieve us. We'll give them a quick brief of our numbers and anything important that has happened during our shift; then we'll hop into the truck and be driven back to our living quarters.

I usually arrive back in my room at about 02:30. I'll then turn on my computer, check my e-mails, and chat with Kendra online for about thirty minutes.

03:00—I'll change into PTs (shorts and a T-shirt), and walk over to the shower trailer to take a shower and brush my teeth. My head usually hits the pillow around 03:45.

As you can see, I only get about 45 minutes of free time a day (15 minutes in the morning and 30 minutes at night).

A couple of times a week, a group of us will sacrifice some sleep and get together to play poker. Games usually last from 03:00 to around 05:30.

Saturdays are my day off. But much of the day is spent doing necessary chores: laundry, haircut, room cleaning, weapons cleaning (M16 & M9), etc. They definitely keep me busy.

Hope all is well. Talk to you later.
Mike

05/23/2006
Iraq Update—Week 39

I've been asked numerous times about how many detainees are at Abu Ghraib, and in the past I've declined from answering believing that such information is classified under OPSEC. I asked the Sergeant of the Guard (SOG) again, and this time he informed me that the overall numbers are public information (not restricted by OPSEC), so here they are: There are approximately 4,700 detainees at Abu Ghraib, guarded by about 130 soldiers at any given time.

In my level, there are a wide variety of personalities. We have all of the juveniles (everyone under the age of 18), and all of the Shias (children and adults). Our detainees range from age 11 to 89, and their education from Ph.D to none at all.

Since we have all of the Shias, it means that every member of the Mahdi Army (al-Sadr's militia) comes to my level. The Mahdi Army is the group of insurgents who battled the Marines in and out of Fallujah and Najaaf; they are the most dangerous, ferocious, and brutal fighters in Iraq (I consider al-Sadr and his army to be the biggest threat to Iraq's future). I'm sure most of you remember those videos of insurgents cutting off the heads of American captives with a sword—we have some of those guys.

A lot of the kids are no angels either, and we have them all: Wahabi, Sunni, Shia, Kurdish, etc. Many of them were IED makers/planters, some were guerrilla fighters—kids grow up quickly in Iraq.

However, I don't have much confidence that all of the detainees designated as insurgents/terrorists by the U.S. Army/Marines are indeed so. We have an 89-year-old man who is both blind and deaf; he is so frail that he is unable to even stand up to come out of the tent for tadot (headcount); according to Military Intelligence (MI) he was an IED trigger-man (the guy who watches convoys drives by and detonates the IED at the precise moment to hit the vehicle) a task that is obviously physically impossible for a blind/deaf man to accomplish.

We also have a detainee whose been labeled a terrorist for possessing "false" police documentation. He was an Iraqi Police Lieutenant in Fallujah and was issued a Fallujah Police Badge. When the insurgency fighting shifted east, he was sent to Baghdad to help maintain order there. In Baghdad he was issued a Baghdad Police Badge. One day, coming out of the Green Zone, a Marine stopped his vehicle and when he was asked for his identification he held up both badges and asked: "Which one would you like to see?" The Marine arrested him for possessing multiple police badges, he's been in Abu Ghraib over 15 months.

Some of the other reasons for detention are even more outrageous. We have two 12-year-old children who were arrested by Marines and have been in Abu over 9 months. Their arrest record (written by the arresting Marines) simply reads "Reason for Arrest: Because we were bored."

So its a strange group, we have some of the most dangerous murderers in the world mixed in with others who were just in the wrong place at the wrong time; and we really have no way of telling them apart; which in a way is good—it forces us to treat everyone equally.

For many of the guards, that means treating everyone equally poorly; most everything that they say to the detainees is either screamed or said in a really condescending tone. They spend the whole day walking around angry. Personally, I'd be miserable if I spent my days that way; I'd much rather joke around and laugh with these people. I think that the other MPs believe they need to yell to demonstrate that they are "in control" (based on examples from prison movies and our Drill Sergeants at Basic Training), but I've found that people generally scream as a method to compensate for NOT really having control of the situation (or at least their own emotions).

I understand that many of these detainees would shove a nail in my throat without hesitation if the opportunity presented itself, and likewise, I would kill any of them if it was necessary to prevent their escape; that is the reality of the situation, but it doesn't mean that we can't be civil to one another. I actually think that doing so makes the job easier, if someone likes you they generally feel a natural desire to want to make you like them too, which makes them much more cooperative. As the old saying goes: "You catch more flies with honey than you do a shotgun."

So I smile and I talk with them. I say "Shaku maku (what's up)" and "Shukrahn (thank you)." Because of this, the detainees have taken to calling me "Sergeant Ze'en (ze'en means "good" in Arabic)." Every day when I walk into the compounds, they'll run up to their fences and ask: "Sergeant Ze'en, Sergeant Ze'en. You my zone today?" If I happen to be their Zone Rep that day, I'll respond: "Yes," and they'll all cheer. If not, I'll say: "La (no)"—for some reason they all understand the English word for yes, but not for no ;)—and they'll let out an, "Ahhhhhhhh."

I notice that they do little things for me to make my job easier that they don't do for the other guards, like being lined up for tadot before I get there, and being in numerical order for ISN# checks, etc. With me, the daily tasks are treated as more of a team/co-operative effort than a fight; and there is still no doubt in anyone's mind that I'm the one in control.

I really don't mind walking around lighting their cigarettes or getting their soccer ball when they ask; the busier I stay, the faster the day seems to go by. Plus, I really find it interesting to talk with them, and I enjoy joking around with the kids.

Sometimes, when I hear the kids calling "Sergeant Ze'en, Sergeant Ze'en, Sergeant Ze'en," I'll duck down behind some sandbags and sneak up to the tent, when I'm right next to them I'll peak my head up and they'll yelp out: "Ah, Sergeant Ze'en!" Then I'll quickly duck back down, and they'll continue again: "Sergeant Ze'en! Sergeant Ze'en!" and I'll pop my head back up; and they'll laugh, and I'll laugh—it's like a game of peek-a-boo.

But being nice is not always easy. A few days ago a boy (around 13 yrs old) collapsed and was unconscious; the other boys in his tent carried him over to the tent sally-port/gate and got their Zone Reps attention. I was the Yard Dog that day, so the Zone Rep called me on the radio, and I ran over to access the situation. We pulled the kid out of the tent and I kneeled down beside him to check for a pulse and breathing (to determine whether I needed to perform CPR). As I bent over the boy's chest, an adult detainee from the adjacent tent came running up to the fence and started screaming at the top of his lungs: "Sergeant! Sergeant! Sergeant! Sergeant! Sergeant! Sergeant!" It was so distracting that I had to stop what I was doing, look up, and say: "Shinu (what)?" He pointed towards that back-side of his tent and said: "Football. Football." (Meaning that he knocked his soccer ball over the fence and wanted me to get it for him.) I'm on the ground, trying to determine whether this child is dead and/or what I can do save him, and there is fat guy in his mid-40s twenty feet away whose only concern is getting his soccer ball back right away. I scream back "Ay Dah (be quiet)." and I point down to the boy and said "Ane Mashgol (I'm busy)." He just looked at me, and continued screaming: "Sergeant! Sergeant! Sergeant! Football! Football! Football!" Now the anger started to build inside of me, but I'm still trying desperately to maintain my composure so that I could properly evaluate the boy. So I looked up and said to him: "Shweyah (not now, wait)." But the guy continues screaming for his soccer ball. I then shouted: "R-ja (get back)! Eskoot (shut up)!" He just ignored my commands and continued screaming. At this point I'm concerned that I'm losing valuable time with the boy trying to get this fat guy to leave me alone. So I looked over to the Zone Rep standing beside me and instructed him to: "Get this fucking guy out of my face." So the Zone Rep went over and got the detainee back into his tent.

The kid ended up being a heat casualty; he had an extremely high heart-rate, and I had to call the trauma team out to resuscitate him. The boy was a Kurd, and the fat adult was a Shia—so he found his soccer ball to be more important than the boy's life. Some of these people are just constantly trying to wear you down and frustrate you, I am continually fighting the urge to retaliate—it's a constant battle. Who knows, maybe over the next few months they'll turn me into an uncaring asshole, too.

One modification that I've made as Yard Dog is that we now do very aggressive shakedowns. It used to be that the guards would just do a quick walkthrough on the randomly selected tent; now we go through everything: every mat, blanket, sandbag, even the tent-liner and seams in the porta-john. We've found some interesting contraband, including a solar powered radio that some of the detainees were using to listen to our radio traffic.

As for what the detainees do here for entertainment, each tent has a soccer ball and they use their clothes-line as a volleyball net. I don't know who taught them how to play volleyball, but they play for hours—some have gotten pretty decent. Of course, they're still constantly hitting the ball over the fence.

There is also a radio that is on for most of the day. There is only one authorized station that we are allowed to play, and even though the station is NEVER changed, they still ask us to change it about 100 times a day. The station plays a mix of Arabic music and American pop. So I'll get to hear the occasional Shakira or Madonna song as I patrol around the yard.

They also watch DVDs for about 5 hours a day. Every four days or so, MI will give us a new DVD (so we have a big collection of new/old ones) containing 2 hours of Iraqi news, a TV show, and a movie, The TV shows range from everything from Iraqi Sitcoms to WWE wrestling to *The Crocodile Hunter*. The movies are generally action/adventure, like: *Top Gun*, *Shrek 2*, and *Armageddon*.

The most popular DVD by far is the one that includes the "Tom and Jerry" cartoon. For some reason the detainees (both the children and the men) love it. There is a Van Damme movie that is also really popular. The detainees also enjoy the 1980s Michael Douglas film *Jewel of the Nile*. There is a scene where Kathleen Turner is dancing with some African Tribal people, and for a few seconds you can catch a glimpse of some topless African woman in the background. They will pause, rewind, and watch that scene in slow-motion over and over for hours.

The day we received the DVD with *Top Gun* I happened to be the Zone Rep for the zone which contained our biggest, baddest, meanest detainee. As I walked by, I noticed that they were all really into the movie; so as the film approached the point were Goose (Tom Cruise's best friend in the film) dies, I hung back to watch and see what their reaction would be (the character was, after all, a U.S. pilot). Well, as Goose laid lifeless in the ocean, I saw our "bad-ass" detainee's eyes start to redden, then well up in tears. Seconds later when it was revealed that Goose didn't make it, the detainee whimpered out, "La (no), La (no)". He then noticed I was watching him, and scurried off into his tent. I guess that goes to show that even the baddest terrorists still have a heart.

Hope all is well. Talk to you later.
Mike

05/30/2006
Iraq Update—Week 40

We have an odd collection of detainees, sometimes I think that our level would make a good sitcom or maybe a circus sideshow.

We have a midget and a guy with only one arm; we also have a detainee (in his mid-50s) who has no fingers on his left hand. At a public event years back, he decided it would be a good idea to show his disapproval for Saddam Hussein by flicking him "the bird;" Saddam had his henchmen hold him down and cut off his fingers.

Since it's hard for us to remember all of the ISN# for these detainees (and most of their names are either really similar or difficult to pronounce), we've given them little nicknames to help us identify them when speaking to each other. Here are a few:

Spanky—reminds us of the character in "The Little Rascals."

Mexico—looks like he's Mexican.

Chunk—reminds us of the character from *The Goonies.*

50—short for 50-Cent. Whenever hip-hop comes on the radio, he'll throw his hands in the air and ask us to turn up the music.

Cyclops—is missing an eye.

Jesus—looks like a dark-skinned Jesus of Nazareth.

Scarface—has a huge scar down the side of his face.

Chewey—about 6'5" 280 pounds, long hair and a scraggly beard, looks like Chewbacca from *Star Wars.*

One aspect of my job that I really find interesting is that I spend my days surrounded by terrorists and insurgents. I've found that if they see that I'm genuinely interested in their opinions (that I'm not angry or judgmental) that I can causally direct the conversation with subtle questions, and get their honest perspective on just about anything. I enjoy listening to them, so I don't say very much, which helps ensure that I never divulge any personal or occupational information. I'm not an interrogator, it's simply for my own personal interest.

In one tent we have an entire platoon-sized element of the Mahdi Army. The leader of this group is very articulate and I think he feels apprehensive about expressing his feelings with the other men in his tent (whom he commands), so seeing me as the only available ear, he's opened up to me on several different occasions.

One time he was very angry, one of the medics who had come by to deliver medication in the morning had called one of the other detainees in his tent a "terrorist." Here is what he said me: "I love my country. Who is this man to come to MY country and call me a terrorist? The Wahabis, the foreigners who come in and hurt my people, yes they are terrorists—but me, I'm trying to build my country with my own two hands. I love my country, just like you love yours."

Americans have a tendency to want to lump our enemies together and blur the lines between insurgent and terrorist. But to the insurgents there is a huge difference between themselves (who are battling a foreign occupier by attacking U.S. troops) and the terrorists (whom are religious extremists killing Iraqi civilians). Every Iraqi that I've encountered (Shia, Sunni, Kurd, etc.), insurgents included, passionately despises Wahhabism (the extreme form of terrorist Islam promoted by al-Qaeda).

Another time, the Mahdi leader had come back from visitation with his mother. He has been in Abu Ghraib for a little over a year, and has 9-month-old son whom he's never met. His mom had brought him some new pictures, and I could see the pride in his eyes as he told me that his boy looked very strong, "like Muhammad Ali." Because security is so poor, his wife is afraid to take their boy on the journey from their home to Abu Ghraib. As he started to describe the situation back home, his pride turned into despair:

"My mother, she was very upset, she was crying. I tried to tell her that I sleep good, I eat, I watch TV; but she doesn't believe me. She hears the name Abu Ghraib and she thinks very bad things happen. I told her she shouldn't worry about me, that I'm worried about them. There has been 147 killings in my city in the past weeks, some with their heads cut off. Outside here it is very bad. The new government I think is good, they fix the courts, they fix the police, but they can't fix the bombs. They can't stop a car bomb. These terrorists, they are ghosts. They're like animals. They kill, and kill, and kill, and kill. No, animals kill for food; these terrorists, they kill for no reason; just for blood. They kill children, they kill old woman—they don't care. It's like a jungle. Iraq, my country, is a jungle, and what can I do? Nothing." When he was finished talking, he thanked me for listening. Sometimes, it seems that all they really want is for someone to listen to them.

Most of the other detainees are nowhere near as articulate. Iraq has a 40% literacy rate (compared with 97% in America), and if 60% can't read (in any language) there are obviously very few people who can communicate effectively in a foreign tongue (like English).

The lack of literacy is a big problem for many of the detainees. When they come back from court, they receive a handful of documents informing them of the status of their case (written in both English and Arabic). Even if the detainee happens to be able to read, these documents often contain complex terms that very few of them can understand.

The real kicker is that if a detainee objects to the courts rulings, they are required to write their own appeal; and even if they are one of the few who is able to read the documents, none of them has an understanding of Iraqi law. So their appeals end up just saying the Arabic equivalent of things like: "No this wrong" or "No, I not do this." Not very persuasive legal arguments, to say the least.

For the detainees who ask, I've taken it upon myself to go around explaining the documents in terms they can understand. So at least now they can know the status of their case—which has helped alleviate some of the frustration that many of them had felt from having no idea as to what was going on.

Unfortunately, this does nothing to help those that are here by an appeal of the arresting unit. If the court rules that the detainee is not guilty of any crime (that they were arrested for no reason), the U.S. Army/Marine unit that initially arrested the detainee can file an appeal (which they almost always do), and the detainee will continue to be held for another six months while more "evidence" is gathered. At the end of those six months, the detainee will go back before the court, and if they are again found not guilty, the arresting unit can appeal again, and the process continues indefinitely. So, that's a big reason why we have innocent people locked up here for years on end.

Which means that there is no real due process here. Maybe that was necessary during major combat operations, when we were advancing through a fog of war, but we are now 3 years removed from that phase of the conflict, and I see absolutely no reason why these people shouldn't be treated fairly. After all, we are supposed to be the ones providing the example of how a legitimate government works. The Iraqis are watching and learning from us; and it makes me ashamed that we are providing such a poor example. Our behavior is morally offensive and there is really no reason for it.

The term the detainees use for being set free is: "Go happy bus." Last week I had this frail little 11 year old boy run up to me with court papers in hand. He asked "Sergeant Ze'en! Sergeant Ze'en! This mean I go happy bus?"

I read over his documents. It was the standard text saying that while the ICCC (court) found him not guilty, the arresting Army unit is appealing, and he will go back before the court again at a later date.

So I had to crush the hopes of this small smiling child by saying: "La (no). Court says enta Ze'en (you're good). But U.S. Army says enta mushkilla (you're a problem). So you stay at Abu Ghraib for 6 (holding up my fingers) more months. Then back to court."

The boy looked down and I could tell that he understood the jist of what I was saying. He then looked back up and asked: "Sergeant Ze'en, do YOU think ane mushkilla (I'm a problem)?" I handed his papers back to him and said: "La (no). I think enta ze'en (you're good)." He then smiled and ran back to play soccer with the other children in his tent.

As I'm sure most of you are aware, Kendra is having surgery in about a week. I've been granted 15 days of emergency leave to come home, be with her, and help her recuperate. I'm very grateful that my unit is allowing me this time to be with her and Morgan. My e-mails will resume upon my return back to Abu Ghraib (in about 3 weeks or so).

Hope all is well. Talk to you later.
Mike

07/11/2006
Iraq Update—Week 46

Well, I'm back from emergency leave. I arrived at Abu Ghraib the evening of Friday, July 7, and was back working in the compounds the next afternoon.

While I was gone, my squad had been rotated to a different level. Now we are guarding the worst of the worst: Wahabis, Takfiris, Salafists, foreign fighters (coming from various Middle Eastern, African, and European nations), and those who have been convicted and are awaiting transfer. I can't get into precisely who we have or where they come from, but we are dealing with some extremely dangerous people.

Ironically, it's actually a little easier working on his level. The facility is set up exactly like the other one (the two are actually connected/adjacent to one another); but for most of our detainees, their ideology gives them such a hatred towards us that they avoid interaction as much as possible. So I no longer have to deal with thousands of repetitious little requests every day.

My company's living quarters have also been moved to a different part of the facility. There isn't as much space in our new area, so I have to share a room with three other soldiers. I was fortunate in that my roommates are guys who I was friendly with prior to our deployment, so we all get along really well with each other.

The weather is about the same as it was when I left: highs are slightly above 120 degrees. It's difficult to describe exactly what it feels like walking around (with full armor) in these high temperatures. Really, the closest comparison is that feeling that you get on your face when you open the door to a hot oven, only this feeling is constant and it covers your entire body. The breeze is actually hot air, so when the wind blows it feels like you are standing next to a massive blow-dryer.

In about a week or so, my squad will be rotated out of the compounds completely. Abu Ghraib is in the process of being closed (with our detainees being transferred to other facilities). As the detainees leave, the infrastructure is being dismantled so that it can be transported to another area of the country. My squad will be on the roads providing security (in up-armored Humvees) for the convoys transporting those materials. The convoy security mission will probably last a few weeks, we don't have any word on what we'll be doing after it's completed.

Yesterday I was sitting in the tower, looking out over a sea of concertina wire, thinking back to the first time I saw those notorious Abu Ghraib torture pictures online. Sometimes I can't believe that I'm actually here. Two years ago I was watching this place in the news, and it was just some abstract location on the other side of the world; now it will be a part of my life forever. I'll be very glad when the last pieces have been moved and this place is no longer in existence.

SGT Ballou is scheduled to leave soon, so the Internet service is going to be taken offline in the next few days. That means that this will be the last regularly scheduled weekly update that I'll be able to send. But, I'll continue typing down my thoughts, and I'll e-mail them out to you guys when I'm in an area with Internet capability.

On a brighter note, my emergency leave went really well (all things considered). Kendra's surgery was a success. It seems that every day she finds new ways to impress me with her strength, thoughtfulness, and love. I am very lucky to have her as my partner in life.

I was able to spend some quality time with Morgan; she's developing quite a vocabulary, I am particularly fond of her animal sounds.

I spent a decent amount of time at the office helping them overcome a few obstacles. I enjoyed getting back into my old grove and being productive in a more cerebral capacity.

I also had the opportunity to attend my 10-year high school reunion. It was good to catch up with some old friends and find out how everyone is progressing with their lives.

It's funny, I can still remember stepping off the bus that first day of my freshman year, standing in awe when I saw just how big those buildings (and the seniors) looked. It's strange to think that it was 14 years ago, and that I was only 14 years old at the time; so in my life, more time has passed since that day than came before it. Where does the time go? It seems that the older I get, the faster time slips away. Hopefully these next 4 months will continue at that accelerated pace.

Hope all is well. Talk to you later.
Mike

07/23/2006
Iraq Update—07/14/2006

Abu Ghraib is the largest U.S. EPW (Enemy Prisoner of War) facility in the world. Thousands of detainees come in and out of here in a month; and the only place where any of this information is recorded is a simple Excel spreadsheet called the "Detainee Tracker." Thousands of names, with ethnicities, medical information, etc., are entered into this spreadsheet; and it is constantly being updated. Anybody who knows anything about Information Systems knows that a spreadsheet is not the proper tool for such a task: there is no history management, no querying or filters, and it's very difficult to maintain at that size. The inability to do searches on medical information has resulted in diabetic detainees not receiving their insulin shots; people (more than one) have literally died because we use such a poor tool.

Several months ago, I volunteered my services to create a simple database which would resolve all of these issues. It's something I could develop in a few hours, give a quick 5-minute class to the data entry personnel, import the information during shift change, and the new app would be up and running seamlessly. Even though this new system would be easier for soldiers to use, be brought on-line without any hassle, and would have actually saved detainee lives, approval was not given for the project.

The only reason why that I can think of is that the old spreadsheet has already been in place for a few years, and our current "leadership" doesn't want to take the responsibility for approving a change. I've seen this unwillingness to make decisions more than once since I've been here.

I think that the problem stems from a lack of leadership experience from the operational officers here on the ground. The Abu Ghraib detention facility is run by the 96th MP BN, which is a California National Guard unit. In the civilian world, the Battalion Commander is actually a security guard, with her only real leadership experience being the two days a month where she works in an office developing a training schedule.

To compound the problem, all the companies placed under the 96th MP BN are also National Guard units, and none of us are actual MP companies; ours was an artillery battery and two of the others were engineering companies.

The Taguba Report (completed in April 2004), which summarized the result/findings of the Army's internal investigations into the 2003 Abu Ghraib detainee abuses, stated that the abuses resulted from the facility being staffed by reservists who were inadequately trained. And yet, the reserve MPs who operated the facility during that time period had significantly more MP training than the reserve artillerymen/engineers who are currently working here (including the officers who are making the operational decisions).

I find the Army's staffing decisions at Abu Ghraib (one of the most important facilities in the world) to be completely baffling. I don't understand why there aren't actual MPs here operating the facility. You'd think that they would at least bring one experienced active duty MP company to provide operational oversight for the untrained reservists. But, instead they keep the trained active-duty MPs stationed at the big bases in Baghdad literally writing speeding tickets to soldiers who drive their Humvees too fast on post; which demonstrates just where the Army places detainee treatment in their list of priorities.

I have plenty of examples of problems resulting from a lack of leadership knowledge. I'll start off with detainee mail. The Geneva Convection states: "Prisoners of war shall be allowed to send and receive letters and cards." However, when I arrived at Abu Ghraib nowhere in the SOP (standing operating procedure) was there any process developed for detainees to send letters or cards.

After my letter to the Battalion Commander last December, the SOP was modified to include a "procedure" for "outgoing mail," granting detainees the right to send "two letters and four cards per month." But when I started working in the compounds (4 months later), it was obvious that nobody had been briefed on the new procedures, so while a process was in the books it was completely unknown within the Internment Facility (IF).

When I asked the detainees if they would like to write letters home, they all jumped at the opportunity. But when I radioed up to the Control Point (CP) requesting POW Mail Forms, the CP responded that they had "no clue what I was talking about." Later that day, I walked up to the CP, grabbed their copy of the SOP, and opened it up to the appropriate section. They again responded that they had never heard of this before, and radioed the request up to the Main Control for clarification. Main Control had also never heard of this procedure, but promised they would look into it and get back to me.

Every day for the next six days I radioed up to CP requesting mail forms, and every day they passed the request up to Main Control. I guess Main Control finally got tired of hearing my requests because on the seventh day they had an answer for me, they told me to have the detainees write their messages on a Red Cross Form, and they would handle it from there.

I knew that this was not correct. Red Cross Forms are only used when the detainee is initially captured so that the Red Cross can ensure that the detainee's family is notified of their whereabouts. And besides, everyone here knows that the

Red Cross is completely incompetent; none of the detainees whom I've spoken with have ever had a Red Cross message actually delivered to their family (and some have been here over 2 years). Heck, under international law, the Red Cross is required (and has been asked by the U.S. Army numerous times) to inspect POW facilities, yet in all the time I've been at Abu Ghraib (and at least six months prior) NO Red Cross representative has ever bothered to come here. Their excuse is that it is "too dangerous"—despite the fact that the Jeb Bush toured the facility two months ago and country singer Toby Keith was here 8 months prior.

So on my day off I read through AR 190–8, the Army Regulation governing EPWs (Enemy Prisoners of War) published October 1997, and it clearly states: "EPWs will use DA Form 2667-R (Prisoner of War Mail (Letter)) and DA Form 2668-R (Prisoner of War (Post Card)) for correspondence," and I found a copy of both forms in the Appendix of that AR. So, I printed up a copy of both forms and handed them into the Control Point. The Control Point had again never heard of them, and passed them up to the IF Commander for him to review prior to my handing them out to the detainees.

The next day, the Interment Facility (IF) Commander responded that he had never seen nor even heard of those forms and that approval would have to be gained from a higher echelon before I could distribute them to the detainees. Of course, the fact that the IF Commander had never heard of the forms shows that he's never bothered to read the Army Regulation governing EPWs. While I was aware that none of the other guards had ever read AR (or Geneva Convention), I was startled to find that the man making the bulk of the command decisions was also ignorant of the most basic Army Regulations.

Unfortunately this was not an isolated incident. The next week a similar problem happened with the Detainee Library. In re-reading the SOP, I noticed that library procedures had been established enabling the detainees to check out books to read, but again nobody working inside of the compounds was notified. So I had to show the SOP to the Control Point and do a weeks forth of daily requests to acquire the appropriate book request forms.

The most egregious example may be that when I first arrived, the detainees had gone weeks without receiving Detainee Request and Complaint Forms (the forms that enable them to make requests and report abuses) despite dozens of detainee solicitations for them every day. When I radioed the Control Point asking for the forms, they notified me that their copy machine was broken and that they were unable to produce them. I requested the forms every day for my first 8 days in the compounds. Finally, I personally went to the IF Commander and informed him that this was a serious violation of the SOP and that I needed those forms immediately; I had them within the hour, and they've been available ever since.

Nobody here seems to understand why I go through these efforts to ensure that the detainees receive proper treatment. But, I personally find it unacceptable for these people to suffer simply because my "leadership" refuses to make the effort to read the appropriate documentation. It saddens me that some of these people have been unable to communicate with their wives and children for years, simply because the Army doesn't care enough to perform proper training/staffing, and the Red Cross bureaucrats are too lazy to do their job.

Insurgencies cannot exist without support from the public, and the vast majority of these detainees will eventually be released back into the population; which I think makes our treatment of them one of the most important factors in bringing stability back to Iraq—this is our opportunity to show them the decency of America and democratic institutions. But, while the U.S. Armed Forces seem to be really good at killing people, we are very poor at winning hearts and minds (and demonstrating decency); we seem to be intent on proving the terrorists/insurgents correct with our cruel indifference.

Hope all is well. Talk to you later.
Mike

P.S. Since I no longer have regular access to the Internet, I'm putting the date that these e-mails were written in the subject line. That way, when I send out a bunch of them, you can read them in order.

07/23/2006
Iraq Update—07/17/2006

In the effort to close Abu Ghraib, it appears that higher echelons have finally come to the conclusion that since there are not enough other facilities to house all of the detainees here, the time has come to release most of the detainees whom the ICCC (court) have found innocent (and are only still detained because U.S. Army/Marine appeals).

About half of the detainees (many of whom I've mentioned in past e-mails) have been set free. Watching the blind/deaf man be carried to the "happy bus" by the other detainees, knowing that he will get to see his family again, and that his life will not needlessly end in the squalor of Abu Ghraib, was one of best moments I've had here.

But there is one man whom will probably be in U.S. custody until the end. He is my age, maybe a couple of years older, and is a Christian from the Kurdish region of northern Iraq (known as Kurdistan to those who live there). After graduating from High School, he acquired a student visa to go to college in the United States, and he received his bachelor's degree from the University of Michigan in just under 4 years.

After college graduation, he returned to Iraq, and after 2 years' of study, received his master's from the University of Baghdad. He then returned back to his native land of Kurdistan to begin his career in business.

A little-known fact is that about a year before our invasion of Iraq: U.S. Special Forces were operating in Kurdistan (northern Iraq). He met a group of them while they were there, and they asked him to come on board as an interpreter (he speaks seven different languages, and his English is flawless—he hardly even has an accent). Seeing an opportunity to avenge the genocide that Saddam had attempted on his people, he accepted their offer, was issued a U.S. Army uniform, body armor, Kevlar helmet, 9 mm pistol, and shotgun; and was flown south to be a part of the very first wave to invade Iraq.

As U.S. Forces pushed north towards Baghdad, he was made the "point man" for house raids (the guy who busts down the door), and would act as interpreter for the on-the-spot interviews/interrogations.

It didn't take long for Baghdad to fall, and the statues of Saddam began to be toppled across the country. In the midst of this, he got word that his mother was missing, apparently kidnapped from her home in the middle of the night. A few days later he received an anonymous call from the kidnappers demanding that he cease working with U.S. forces; otherwise they would decapitate her. He refused.

A week later news arrived that his mother's headless corpse had been found on the side of the road; he tells me that at that moment he pledged to dedicate his life to the elimination of terrorism. He was unable to attend his mother's funeral. It was around this time that he began dating a female U.S. Army Specialist in the unit to which he was attached.

A few months later, as the war shifted from invasion to occupation, his unit's mission changed from house-raids to traffic checkpoints (with vehicle searches), and he continued working with them as an interpreter out in the streets of Baghdad. As the attrition of life in Iraq began to wear on the U.S. soldiers in his unit, jealousy of his relationship with the American girl (I hear she was very attractive) began to brew; and one day, the commander of the U.S. Army Brigade to which he was attached called him into his office and ordered him to cease dating her. Being that an Iraqi translator is not actually an enlisted soldier, he was not required to comply with the order, and he informed the Brigade Commander that he was declining to obey with the directive. At that point the Brigade Commander could have terminated the interpreter's contract with the Army, or he could have ordered the female soldier to end the relationship; he chose to do neither, I guess the anger of being "disobeyed" by an Iraqi planted the seed of a different course of action in his mind.

Two days later, during a typical day stopping traffic, after finishing questioning the driver of a suspicious vehicle, the interpreter looked up to see that the rest of his U.S. Army company was nowhere to be found. He had been abandoned in one of the worst sections of Baghdad, wearing a U.S. Army uniform with an American Flag on his shoulder; basically left there to be killed. Luckily he saw an Iraqi Police (IP) car nearby. Unluckily, it was nearly 6 blocks away and the area was swarming with anti-coalition forces.

He had gone less than 2 blocks before the first shot rang out, the bullet striking him directly in the back, lodging into his body armor. The impact of the round knocked him off of his feet, but within seconds he had drawn his 9 mm pistol and was back on his feet running towards the IP vehicle.

He made it another block and a half, then he was struck with 5 more rounds: 1 was stopped by the armor, but the other 4 hit their mark (3 going into his abdomen and 1 through his shoulder). As he laid on the ground bleeding, with his life quickly draining from his body, he tells me that his mind was again filled with thoughts of his mother, and that gave him the strength to pull his bullet-riddled body back to his feet and run the remaining two and a half blocks to the IP vehicle; he collapsed unconscious at the feet of a young Iraqi policeman.

He awoke two days later in the bed of an Iraqi hospital. The doctor told him that the Iraqi policeman had called an ambulance which had brought him there, that his heart had stopped twice on the way to the hospital, and that barring infection he would survive (though they had to remove one of his kidneys).

During his recovery, he was visited by an Iraqi reporter. The fact that a U.S. interpreter was being treated in an Iraqi hospital (instead of a U.S. military facility) was unusual, and the reporter was interested in the details behind the story. The interpreter told about his girlfriend, the meeting with the Brigade Commander, and being left for dead. The story (including the names of everyone involved) was published in an Arabic newspaper a few days later. Within a week, the Brigade Commander whom had been named in the story filled out a sworn statement claiming that the interpreter was a "terrorist," and that was all that it took to have him sent to Abu Ghraib.

When he arrived here he was thrown in the Special Housing Unit (SHU) for 14 days, where as a "terrorist" he was routinely subjected to the torture of being strapped in-between medical litters and tied down into a restraint chair in the hot sun for hours on end. The U.S. soldiers felt justified in inflicting this torment on the freshly wounded and recovering former-Army interpreter, because the orders to do so were signed directly by a U.S. Army Colonel (his former Brigade Commander).

When the two weeks were completed, he was thrown into the general population where numerous attempts were made on his life by other detainees; not only was he a non-Arab Christian in the same cage with Sunni Arab insurgents, but he was actually assigned to the same tent with 2 detainees who he personally arrested while working with U.S. forces.

He tells me that every day in the general population was a battle for his life, but motivated by the memory of his mother, he continued to survive. A few months went by, and the U.S. Army/Marines began capturing more and more foreign terrorists. Many of these terrorists spoke Pashtu (the language of Afghanistan), not Arabic; which created a big problem since there are no Pashtu interpreters stationed here. However, Pashtu is one of the languages that the detained former-interpreter speaks, so military intelligence would use him to translate notes/writing that were confiscated from the foreign detainees. After a while (about 14 months ago), it was decided that he was too valuable of a resource to be left to die in the general population, and they moved him into the Shia level where I was later assigned.

He was in Abu Ghraib for almost two years and had never been permitted to go before the court or even speak to a lawyer (the U.S. Army claims that he has top-secret information that they don't want him to reveal), and the only witness against him continues to be his former Brigade Commander (who was rotated out of Iraq over a year ago).

So here he sat in his yellow jumpsuit, treated just like every other thug we have detained here. I only ever heard him complain one time, and that was in regards to our records having him listed as a terrorist. This is what he said to me:

"A terrorist? How can I be a terrorist? They killed my mother, they tried to kill me (showing me he scars), if the U.S. government want to hold me here for no reason, then fine, say that; but don't call me a terrorist."

Personally, I don't see how military intelligence can label him a terrorist and then trust him to translate writings seized from other terrorists. It just doesn't make any sense. But, we all know (me, him, and the U.S. Army) that because there are orders signed by a Colonel, he will be detained until U.S. troops finally leave Iraq.

While I was away on leave, we had several large detainee transfers to Camp Bucca (a detention facility in southern Iraq). He was on one of them. When he arrived at Bucca, he was thrown back into the general population area of the facility. It wasn't long before he was recognized by some of the other detainees; and a few days later, he was beaten nearly to death. He had to be helicoptered out to one of the main hospitals in Iraq, where he is currently lying on a cot in stable condition.

Before I went on leave, I asked him that after all my country has done to him, why does he continue to help us by translating intelligence documents. He told me that he still "loves the U.S. Army," because we "kill the terrorists every day," and that he's proud to be able to continue working to fulfill the pledge that he made to himself to eliminate terrorism after the death of his mother. He's a better man than me.

Hope all is well. Talk to you later.
Mike

07/23/2006
Iraq Update—07/19/2006

Well, the detention facility at Abu Ghraib is now closed. On Sunday (July 16), I was in charge of a large portion of one of the final big detainee transfers. Our Detainee Operations mission has been fatiguing; I was glad to see the detainees board their helicopters and fly away to become someone else's problem.

Five hours after the last helicopter took off, I was in the turret of my gun-truck (up-armored Humvee) headed down the road on the first convoy of our new Convoy Security mission.

The remainder of the detainees were transported to the new facility last night. Working in the compounds ended up being more interesting than I initially thought that it would be; it gave me the opportunity to interact and learn from people whom I would never have been able to come in contact with otherwise.

I think that a lot of Americans have a misconception about Islam in the Middle East—especially within Iraq. People see the images on TV: the bombs, the women in head scarves, the daily prayers; and assume that it is a nation full of religious zealots. My experience with the detainees has shown that not to be so.

For our detainees, who were suspected insurgents (the most likely group to be religious extremists), only half of them even prayed regularly, with about a third following the traditional "call to prayer" 5 times a day (and that is the very most basic practice/tenet of Islam).

Even those who rigidly practice the Islamic faith are not pious men: they smoke, they steal, they lie, etc.

In the Shia level, practically every day we'd have problems with new detainees being assigned to us in the morning, and a few hours into the day begging to be moved to one of the Sunni levels. There is an assumption among some Iraqis that because Shias comprise the majority in the new government, that they are given better treatment at our detention facilities. So upon capture, many Sunnis will lie and claim to be Shia; but once they get to their tent and see that everyone is treated equally poorly, they change their tune—and in the process created a bunch of extra work for the Interpreters and MI (to re-interview them), the DIMS operators (to re-assign them), and the guards (to move them).

In my conversations with detainees, I found that very few were really knowledge in their faith; I actually think that I may know more about the history of Islam than most of them.

During several cultural/religious conversations that I engaged in while working in the Shia level, when the detainees saw that I had a certain level of knowledge in their beliefs, many assumed that I was actually a Muslim. On a few occasions I was asked: "Enta Muslim (you're a Muslim). Shia or Sunni?"; and I replied: "La, Ane la muslim (No, I no muslim)." A couple of times the detainees insisted: "La. Enta Muslim. Enta Muslim. Shia or Sunni?" One time I asked: "Well, which do you think?" Their reply was: "Enta Ze'en (you're good). Enta Shia. (you're Shia)." For a Shia insurgent fighter to label me (their American captor) as a fellow Shia, I consider to be an amazing complement.

While I was home on leave, I was asked my opinion on what percentage of detainees in my level were actually insurgents (i.e., not arrested by marines/soldiers for just "being bored"). Well, about a week before I left, we moved a Mahdi leader (whose conversations I mentioned in a previous e-mail) to another level. As I was escorting him down Dirka-Dirka Blvd., about 75% of adult detainees in the surrounding tents rushed up to the front fence and started chanting the Mahdi "war cry." The chanting lasted for about 10 minutes; when I informed the other guards what the chant meant, none of us were surprised to see that three quarters of our adult detainees were in fact members of the Mahdi Army, the anti-Western, Shia militia. Insurgent attacks against coalition forces are primarily Sunni-driven (where as most of the sectarian/militia violence against Iraqis is orchestrated by Shias); so Sunnis are considerably more likely to be just randomly detained by U.S. forces.

But for most of the Shia, their participation/support for the Mahdi Army stems from pragmatism not ideology. I asked one of the detainees whom I saw engaging in the war chant: "Sistani or Muqtada?" Whether he was a follower of the pro-Western cleric Grand Ayatollah Ali al-Sistani or the anti-Western cleric Muqtada al-Sadr. His response was: "Muqtada," and when I asked him "lee-esh (why)?" he responded: "Sistani sleep for 35 years. Muqtada has patrols, gives security." That seems to be the common reason why Shias flock to al-Sadr: they believe that Sistani didn't do enough to oppose Saddam during his dictatorship (Saddam had him under "house-arrest"). Those who took a more pro-active approach (such as Muqtada's father and brothers) were assassinated. It is also clear that the Iraqi government is not doing enough today to provide security, and while Sistani urges patience while innocent blood is spilled on the streets, al-Sadr has formed militias to take security matters into his own hands.

The Iraqi people yearn for security (survival is the most basic human desire); they are tired of seeing their cousins, brothers, sisters, aunts, uncles, children, etc., killed and maimed—and with the U.S. and Iraqi governments continually failing to protect them, they've had to turn to sectarian militias (i.e., the Mahdi Army) for assistance. But from my perspective, it really looks as though support for those militias comes out of necessity (not choice), so if we can ever get our act together and bring security to these beleaguered areas, support for the sectarian militias will dry up—but that's a big "if."

During the months that I worked in the Shia level, every couple of days I would go around to the tents before wahed-wahed and do a little informal poll about some Iraqi/world leaders to gauge the political leanings of the detainees; this was done merely for my own personal interest. Since there are major infra-structural and security problems prevalent throughout the country, it really isn't possible for a large organization (such as CNN or Zogby) to conduct nation-wide polls; so my personal polls (of a few hundred detainees captured from all over the country) may be one of the best available indicators of public sentiment for Shias (whom comprise about 60% of the population). Though since the detainees are all suspected insurgents, I would imagine that the results were probably more anti-Western than the population on a whole. Still, I found the results to be interesting.

About 25% of the detainees didn't like anyone; they said that anyone involved in politics is an Ali Baba (thief), these are the results of the remaining 75% of those asked:

Saddam Hussein (former Dictator, Sunni)—unanimously (100%) despised, 100% passionately so Jalal Talabani (current President, Kurd)—unanimous dis-liked, but the reaction was no where near as strong as Saddam. While everyone disliked him, nobody seemed to HATE him, there was not a lot of passion in their response.

George W Bush—there was a mixed reaction, about 30% said he was ze'en (good), about 70% said he was muze'en (bad)—but nobody seemed all that pas-sionate in their responses one way or the other. Interestingly, his approval rating with the Shia detainees at Abu Ghraib is about the same as with Americans back home.

Donald Rumsfeld—unanimously (100%) despised, 100% passionately so. He ranks right up there with Saddam, and I can certainly understand why.

The most entertaining response that I received was when I asked them their opinion on Condoleezza Rice: about 70% responded with indifference, the other 30% of the detainees (across various tents) jumped up, started gyrating their pel-vis, and saying "feeky-feeky, feeky-feeky" (I don't think that requires a transla-tion).

I noticed a slight shift over the 6 weeks that I conducted these polls in regards to their opinions of Jaafari, Maliki, and al-Sadr; which I think further demon-strates the pragmatic nature of the Iraqi people. As the new government began to coalesce and develop, I started to see support firm up for the more secular political leaders:

Ibrahim al-Jaafari (former Prime Minister, backed by al-Sadr, Shia)—initially everyone pretty much approved of him, but with no real passion in anyone's responses.

Nouri al-Maliki (current Prime Minister, more moderate, Shia)—initially there was a very mixed reaction. Overall, I'd say there were more people who dislike him than liked him, but there was still no real passion.

By the end of my polling: the reactions to Jaafari and Maliki had swapped. Maliki now had majority (non-passionate) approval and Jaafari had the mixed reaction. The detainees must have been seeing things on the news or getting reports from back home during family visitation that were causing them to rethink their prior political opinions.

Muqtada al-Sadr (Shia cleric)—Initially: about 70% passionately adored him. At the end: still with about 70% approval, but only about half of them still respond with that same kind of passion.

Whenever I asked about al-Sadr, at least a couple of detainees would come up and ask me if I personally like him. My response was always the same: I'd smile and say, "I don't know, but I know that he doesn't like me." It got a laugh every time.

Hope all is well back home. Talk to you later.
Mike

07/26/2006
Iraq Update—07/25/2006

I've been pretty busy lately; my new schedule doesn't afford me any days off. We escort two big convoys every day, and when we arrive at our destination, we are usually tasked out for additional smaller escort missions in the surrounding Baghdad area.

I am the gunner for Delta Team, which provides rear security for the convoys. This task requires a 180-degree shift in mindset from detainee operations. Now, my main responsibility is essentially to kill anyone who threatens the convoy.

Virtually everything regarding convoys (tactics, movements, etc.) is guarded by OPSEC. So I won't be able to provide any information on my activities until we conclude this mission.

It is indescribably hot and dusty up in the turret, and the days are long. But we all still prefer this over working in the compounds.

Hope all is well. Talk to you later.

Mike

P.S. I attached some pics. The first one is of me in the turret of my gun-truck. The second was taken by another soldier riding along with our convoy.

08/04/2006
Iraq Update—07/27/2006

When I think back on my time in the compounds, what seems to have left the biggest impression on me are the detained children.

Though they were here for being suspected of supporting the insurgency, these kids were still kids—and they acted like it.

I remember one time they tore all of the cotton lining out of their jackets, attached it to their face (making what looked like white beards), and marched around their tent saying: "Sergeant! Sergeant! We are hajjis (the term for a wise old man), you must let us go."

They would constantly makes faces (and stick out their tongues) through the fence at the other kids detained in adjacent tents.

They would also collect the mud surrounding their tent, mold it into different little objects (cars, tanks, people, etc.), and leave them in the sun to dry/harden. Some of the mud toys that they made were pretty impressive. They once gave me a jeep that actually had working wheels (made entirely of mud) that would roll across the ground.

Very few of the kids knew their birthdays or even how old they were. The responsibility of assigning ages fell to the soldiers working in the hospital. I don't know what criteria they used to determined how old the detainees were, but we had some kids that looked to be 11 years old labeled as 17 (and vice-versa).

Periodically, higher echelons would pick 50 or so Sunni kids, decide that they had all turned 18, and send them to one of the adult levels. Some of them look like they were still middle-schoolers; and I'm sure that most of them ended up being abused by the adults.

Rape was not uncommon among the detainees in the Sunni levels; MI had been able to determine that the price for one of the newly transferred kids was 22 cigarettes.

With the closing of the Abu Ghraib detention facility, the vast majority of our juveniles were released. While they were here, their living conditions were no better than that of the adults. Thousands of kids have come through Abu Ghraib; they are the future of Iraq, and I doubt that they left here with a very positive impression of America.

Many of the adult detainees acted like children as well. Sometimes it really felt like I was just babysitting these people.

The detainees would constantly make "yogurt"—they'd leave bottles of milk in the hot sun for about a week (until it curdled and chunks formed) and then eat/drink it. Of course, it would make many of them sick. Every time we did shakedowns, we'd end up removing dozens of these bottles. But they'd just keep on making it—their reasoning: "We like it Sergeant. Yogurt ze'en (good)! Yogurt ze'en!"

They would also fake injuries. One time I had a detainee run up to me clutching his arm and screaming: "Sergeant! My arm broke! My arm broke!" So, I called the Yard Dog on the radio and asked him to come over to access the situation. When the Yard Dog arrived (about 10 minutes later), we walked over to the tent and saw that the "injured" detainee was playing volleyball. After watching him play for a few minutes (following a decent spike for a point), we went over to the fence and asked him how his arm was feeling. He laughed, but then as we began to walk away, he grabbed it again and whaled: "Arm broke! Arm broke!"

The detainees seemed to enjoy harassing us for no reason. A typical example:

A detainee would yell "Sergeant! Sergeant! Sergeant! I need soap! I need soap!" So I'd grab a few bars of soap, walk over to the tent and hand them to him. Then a few minutes later, he'd be at it again "Sergeant! Sergeant! Sergeant! I need soap! I need soap! I need soap!" So I'd open the gate, walk into his tent, point at the pile of soap in the corner, and ask "Lee-esh (why) more?" My question would always receive the same response: A blank stare, a shrug of the shoulders, and a dejected "I don't know."

A few months back, the chow detail returned from the dining facility with a bottle of sparkling grape juice. One of the other guards and I were sharing it as we patrolled down Dirka-Dirka Blvd. About a third of the way down the road, one of the detainees called us over and asked: "Is that alcohol?" The other guard responded: "Yeah, right." I guess the detainee either didn't believe him or he didn't catch the sarcasm, because he then looked around and asked: "Let me have some?" We chuckled, and the guard answered: "OK, if you think you can handle it."

The other guard poured some into an empty water bottle and handed it to him through the gate. The detainee took a little sip, his eyes widened, and he exclaimed: "Whoooh! Whoooh! That's like whiskey, man! Whoooh!" I asked: "So you think it's strong?" The detainee answered: "Yeah, man." I ended the exchange by saying: "Alright, well enjoy yourself," and we continued on with our patrol. About 30 minutes later when I walked by his tent again, I saw the detainee stumbling around like he was drunk. I never did have the heart to tell him that it was just grape juice.

Hope all is well. Talk to you later.
Mike

08/04/2006
Iraq Update—08/01/2006

Today is my little girl's 2nd birthday. I was able to find one of the last remaining phones on the FOB (everything is being dismantled/removed as this place closes), so I got to hear Morgan's tiny voice again—I think that "Hi Dada" might very well be the two sweetest words in the English language.

I saw a few pictures of her birthday party—more memories missed. Sometimes I feel like I'm really failing my family. I've turned Kendra into a single mother, deprived Morgan of her father, and put my parents through emotional anguish. But even with everything that I know now, I still think that enlisting was the right thing to do. I have supported from its inception and still support today the policy that has lead our country into Iraq—and it would be hypocritical for me to ask another American to do something that I am not willing to endure myself.

As you all know, I voted for President Bush in 2004, and that was in large part because I believe it is necessary to remain here in Iraq until the newly elected government can secure this nation on their own. I really don't think it will take much longer; I can see light at the end of the tunnel. Every few days I notice more Iraqi Police manning checkpoints—hopefully they'll have better luck at quelling the violence than we have. I would be surprised if Iraq were not responsible for the security of the entire country by this time next year (with the U.S. acting in a supporting capacity), putting them in full command of their own destiny, and allowing us to begin large troop reductions.

Even now, our troop levels are misleading. There are roughly 130,000 troops in Iraq; but of those, only about 10% are actually in any real danger. Those stationed at small FOBs in rough parts of town have the threat of mortars and sniper fire, and those out in the streets have to deal with the IEDs and small-arms fire. But, the vast majority of soldiers are tucked away on large safe camps like Liberty or Stryker, doing regular jobs like mail clerk, finance admin, or various FOB details.

Soldiers doing this type of work are called POGs (pronounced pOg, like rogue): Personnel Other than Grunt. The may be deployed in a war zone, but they aren't really in the war. They don't wear their IBA (Abu Ghraib is the only FOB in Iraq where soldiers are required to wear armor), they don't carry ammunition for their weapons, they've certainly never been shot at or have to point their rifle at another man and make the decision whether it's necessary to pull the trigger.

They work a 9-to-5 job, eat McDonalds for lunch, watch satellite TV after work, and go out fishing or to a movie on the weekends. I imagine that life for them in Iraq isn't all that different than back in the states.

It seems to me that right now there are way too many POGs here and nowhere near enough Grunts. There have been times when my squad has had to push 30-vehicle convoys with only four gun-trucks (the standard is six); meanwhile at any of the BIAP dining facilities there is always one soldier checking IDs and five others just standing around watching him (I guess they take turns over their 8 hr. shift). Troop levels could easily be reduced by the thousands by just sending home the superfluous POGs.

It's easy to tell when you're in POGs-ville, all you have to do is look for the threatening signs warning soldiers of things that those really in war are not concerned with; such as: a reminder that wearing headphones in uniform is against army regs, or a stern warning about the dangers of shoplifting.

Every day, we drop off trucks at one of the big POG Army camps. I attached a picture of me standing in front of one of their signs—unfortunately, the beer is non-alcoholic.

Hope all is well. Talk to you later.
Mike

BEWARE!
Violation of General Order # 1 is very serious !
Is drinking alcohol worth this happening to YOU ?
REPORT CRIME to
MILITARY POLICE
DSN: 822-4790 IRAQNA: 0790-194-2960
U.S. ARMY

08/15/2006
Iraq Update—08/07/2006

We only have about a week of convoy missions left. Everything is going alright, though this time in the turret has been rough on my knees and back. I walk out of my room every morning smelling like a medicine cabinet: sunblock, Gold Bond, Chapstick, Suave lotion (for my eczema), Preparation H, and Icy Hot; anything to make it through another day.

We've been pushing two convoys a day (sometimes four), escorting approximately 25 KBR semi trucks. Each convoy takes about 50 minutes from start-point to end-point. The trucks are all driven by Iraqi day laborers. They're hauling away the remains of the U.S. presence at Abu Ghraib: bunkers, t-barriers, shipping containers, generators, razor wire, etc.

The Iraqi drivers are absolutely horrendous, reckless really. It's not unusual for them, in the middle of a convoy, to just stop, pull over to the side of the road, and get out of their truck to grab something from behind the cab. Other times they'll lag back, leaving a big gap between themselves and the truck in front of them (to the point that we lose sight of the rest of the convoy).

These roads are not safe, and their actions force me to further expose myself as our truck leaves its position so that I can hang out of the turret and yell at them to correct whatever problem they're creating. Every day they do at least one thing that causes me to ask: "What the fuck is wrong with these people?"

The insurgents have been pretty busy on our route over the past few weeks. Our record is currently 21 IEDs in a 48-hour period (11 IEDs on 30 JUL, 10 IEDs on 31 JUL). I don't think that there is any other place in Iraq that can match that level of activity. We have at least 2 IEDs and 2 small arms attacks on our route every day, along with the occasional RPG strike and frequent sniper fire.

They can be rather clever with their IED placement. One time there was a dead dog left on the side of the road with a 135 mm. IED stuffed in its body. Fortunately a gunner sensed something was wrong (dead dogs are a common site), trusted his gut, and they cordoned off the road as EOD came to the site to inspect the carcass and perform a controlled detonation.

The roads that we use are scarred with giant holes from years of IED explosions. It is very common for insurgents to put pressure-plated IEDs in these holes and cover them with gravel, leaving what looks like a regular pothole. Since running over these "potholes" can have deadly consequences, drivers are instructed to avoid hitting them at all costs. During some stretches of our route it looks like our convoy is going through a long slalom.

On August 1st after arriving at our destination, we were assigned a secondary mission of escorting a small convoy of three vehicles through an Iraqi checkpoint in what is widely considered the most dangerous section of Baghdad. There were two gun-trucks providing security, one in the front, and us in the rear. It was late afternoon when the sun is at its hottest, and as usual for that time of the day the streets were packed with cars.

We arrived at the checkpoint and came to a stop so that the Iraqi Police could inspect the trucks we were escorting. Several seconds later, a civilian car came driving directly towards our 6 o'clock. At around 80 meters I motioned for him to stop. His vehicle came to a halt at about 50 meters. As soon as the wheels stopped, the door flung open, and a man in his early 40s jumped out of the driver's seat and began walking towards my gun-truck at a rapid pace.

I immediately straightened up in the turret, held up my hand, and yelled "Stop! Ogoff!" The man, unfazed, continued walking towards me.

I pick up my M-16 and yelled "Get Back! R-ja!" The man, now about 35 m away, slowed down his pace, but continued towards my vehicle.

He pointed behind me and yelled back: "Mister, I must talk to someone!"

I responded: "No! La! Get Back! R-ja!"

He replied: "Mister, I go speak to him," and continued walking towards me.

He was now only about 30m away. I raised the M-16 to my cheek, took aim at his chest, and said: "Stop or I'll shoot! Ogoff terra armee!"

The man continued walking forward.

He was about 25m away, still moving forward, when I put my finger on the trigger and yelled out my final warning: "Get Back! R-ja!"

This is what was running through my mind:

"If he has a stick of dynamite strapped to his chest, how close would be have to be to kill me? What if he had two sticks? Shit! He's already too close."

Before pulling the trigger, one last thought flashed into my head: my daughter blowing out two candles on her birthday cake.

I made a final wish: "Please, don't make me kill you. Not on my daughter's birthday."

It's as if he heard me telepathically, because just as I began to squeeze, the man suddenly stopped, shrugged his shoulders, turned around, walked back to his car, and drove away.

I'm still not sure that he realized just how close he had come to being killed. On any other day, he would have run out of time; he would be dead. It was the thought of forever staining my daughter's special day that allowed him the extra fraction of a second to change his course of action. Morgan saved his life.

Hope all is well. Talk to you later.
Mike

08/15/2006
Iraq Pictures—08/07/2006

I attached pictures to show you two different IEDs going boom. These were controlled dets—which is how the cameras were poised and ready to capture the explosions. In both of these cases, the lead gunner spotted the IED, we cordoned off the road, and called EOD who brought out one of their robots to set off the IED.

08/15/2006
Iraq Update—08/11/2006

There is an image that for some reason I can't seem to shake from my mind. On the 8th of August, early in the morning, on our usual daily route, I saw a girl standing among a bunch of sheep. She looked to be about 9 years old, with olive skin and long brown hear. She was wearing a green dress, and she waved to me as our convoy rolled passed. I was struck by how beautiful she was, not in a sensual way, but something around her eyes, an innocence that I haven't seen in quite some time. I didn't think that it could exist in this land so scared with war, death, and occupation—I doubt that it will survive in her much longer. Innocence, the uncounted casualty of war.

I've heard a lot of war stories, I've read many books and seen quite a few movies on the subject; and I've now had the opportunity to experience war first-hand. From my perspective, there is something that all of the depictions get profoundly wrong: everything that I've seen and read has in some way romanticized armed conflict. Even when the "horrors" are portrayed, it is done with a sense of reverence.

Here is what I've found: There is nothing honorable about war. War is mass murder for a political cause, nothing more. At best it can be justified, but it should never be glorified.

War is Haditha, where 24 unarmed Iraqis, including women and children (as young as two), were killed by a squad of Marines.

War is Hamdania, where an unarmed civilian was dragged from his home, bound at the hands and feet, and executed by U.S. troops.

War is Mukaradeeb, where 42 civilians (including 11 woman and 14 children) were killed by an American AC-130 Gunship.

War is Mahmudiyah, where five American soldiers gang-raped and murdered a 14-year-old girl after killing her unarmed father, mother, and seven year old sister.

War is Ishaqi, where American forces gathered family members—including 5 children (ages: 5, 5, 3, 3, 6 months), 4 women and 2 men—into a single room, blind-folded, bound, and executed them. They then proceeded to bomb their house, burn three vehicles, and kill their animals.

These incidents are all being reviewed/investigated by the U.S. military; and since these cases have been publicized by the press (despite some military cover-ups), punishments will be inflicted. But one thing should be clear: Atrocities are an inseparable part of war. It seems that every time one of these events is publicized, military brass goes out of their way to portray it as just an isolated incident somehow removed from the everyday routine of our occupation. The reality is that these things are inevitable.

I'm not implying that they should be ignored; granting impunity would encourage more than just the inherent abuses. But let's not feign naiveté. In war, the only real certainty is that innocent people will die; there will always be cruelty. This is why war is often referred to as a "necessary evil." But too often that phrase is used to argue the NECCESSARY while brushing aside the EVIL.

As a nation, we make a deal with our collective conscience that the objective achieved by wagging war is worth the atrocities committed in its execution (a.k.a., the end justifies the means).

We recruit a bunch of teenagers, pump them up with propaganda on how evil the enemy is ("we are fighting them here so that they don't kill our families back home"), dehumanize the Iraqi population ("the hajjis, they live in mud huts, they don't even use toilet paper, they aren't like real people"), give them a bunch of automatic weapons, and dump them into highly populated civilian areas with no real ability to tell the good guys from the bad.

Added on top of that: months of separation from their family, stress from multiple deployments; and then one day a member of their squad is killed. Are we really surprised that some of these kids are going to go out looking for revenge?

The question is: how many dead children is democracy worth? 1, 100, 1,000, 10,000? In Iraq the question is not academic.

How many dead American teenagers? How many killed Iraqi civilians is it worth to bring democracy to this country? How many slaughtered children exactly? Only a madman would say "as many as it takes" (that they would see all Iraqis killed in the effort to bring them "freedom"). For the Commander-in-Chief, this question is not rhetorical; a real formula must be devised so that a proper strategy can be developed and executed. Abraham Lincoln call this the "terrible arithmetic": How many die today (via U.S. and retaliatory insurgent/terrorist attacks) so that others don't have to die in the future (via the hands of a dictator). Reasonable people will invariably differ in opinion, but the decision is ultimately one man's, with history left to judge whether his "arithmetic" makes him a "war hero" or a "war criminal."

But in any event, war should be avoided whenever possible—not be glorified; and I'm not going to perpetuate it's glorification in these e-mails by writing harrowing accounts of combat. But, so that you can better understand some of what goes on here, I've attached a copy of a sworn statement that I was obligated to write [see Appendix H] regarding a small arms incident that occurred several weeks back. It's typical of most small arms attacks on convoys.

Our unit's Rules of Engagement (ROE) prohibit us from engaging the enemy if there is a likelihood of collateral damage, and since our daily route takes us through towns and villages, that risk is almost always prevalent, so the opportunity to return fire is rare. It can be frustrating at times, but I understand the necessity of the restriction; one of insurgent's primary strategies is to bait us into shooting up civilian areas, creating resentment/hostility, and undermining our relationship with the population as a whole.

Hope all is well. Talk to you later.
Mike

08/15/2006
Iraq Pictures—08/11/2006

Here are some more convoy pics.

08/15/2006
Iraq Update—8/14/2006

Yesterday was our last convoy mission. We left Abu at around 7:00 am—never to return again. My company was the last to leave; the Iraqi Army is now in total control of Abu Ghraib. The first Iraqi Humvees rolled through the gates just as we were making our final exit.

In the last weeks, they removed the dining facility (we had to settle for eating MREs), ripped out all of the phones, eliminated the laundry, and even turned off the electricity for long stretches of time.

The place really felt like a ghost town—with everyone else gone, over 90% of it was uninhabited. There were many times that I'd look around and find myself completely alone.

Sometimes after convoys, we'd be tasked out to assist one of the other platoons in demolishing the compounds and various portions of the LSAs. We'd grab some sledge hammers and smash down walls, tearing out anything made of wood. By the time we left, the compounds were completely leveled, it was just flat dirt all the way back to the outer walls. It looked like the facility had never existed—hopefully the memory of what happened there won't be as easily destroyed.

Right now I'm at Camp Stryker. Over the next week, 75% of the company will be flying down to Camp Bucca to continue on with the final months of our deployment. My platoon has been assigned a different mission: We will spend 30 days at Camp Victory (an enormous base in Baghdad) preparing vehicles (e.g., getting increased armor installed, switching out radios, etc.) for a long convoy down to Camp Bucca. The convoy will give me the opportunity to see a large portion of the country. It's a 13-hour drive, so I'm thankful for the 30 days to prepare and rest up for the journey. When we arrive at Bucca, we'll link up with the rest of the company, and assist them until our relieving unit arrives. At that point our mission is complete, and the entire company will fly back to the good ol' US of A.

Hope all is well. Talk to you later.
Mike

09/03/2006
Iraq Update—09/03/2006

The Iraqi Army (IA) abandoned Abu Ghraib twenty-six hours after their initial arrival. We received word on 16AUG at 0945; by 1145 we were packed and on the road headed back to our old home.

Nobody seems to know why they left their post. When I heard the news, my first thought was of Benedict Arnold at West Point—we know that many in the IA have split loyalties with the insurgency, and it would be a big feather-in-their-cap to gain possession of such an infamous facility. Though it may have just been a case of incomprehensible incompetence.

Fortunately we had left a small detachment behind. We returned to find the place undisturbed, and were able to re-occupy the area with minimal effort; I spent the first 36 hours manning a battle position in the northeast corner of the FOB.

On 18AUG my squad resumed daily convoys through western Baghdad. Same route, but instead of escorting KBR trucks, we'd run missions strictly for our unit: take the commander to a meeting, bring supplies/food/water/fuel/laundry back to Abu, etc. It was nice to be rid of the Iraqi truck drivers.

By the end, we'd driven the route about a hundred times, and I felt confident in our abilities to notice anything out of the ordinary. One day, I found myself taking note of a red garment that hung on a clothesline by a house near our destination. It was the first time that I remember seeing any color other than white and black on that particular line. It could have been a signal to the insurgency, or they could have had an unfriendly visitor, or it could've just been a new piece of clothing for a member of their family (which is most likely, since nothing happened); but I remained extra vigilant during that stretch. We pass dozens of clotheslines every day, and I was impressed that my mind had been able to subconsciously capture and process that level of detail. Those little things can be the difference between spotting the IED or having it blow up under your vehicle.

While we did convoys, the rest of the company spent 8 hours a day manning towers along the outer perimeter. Without computers, phones, and mail they went nearly a month with absolutely no contact with their loved ones back home. Being on the convoy team, I was able to make quick calls from our destination to Kendra every few days.

At some point, Abu Ghraib was downgraded from a FOB to an Outpost—whatever that means.

On 20AUG a couple of mortars busted up our living area pretty good. I came close to vomiting from inhaling all of that smoke. There were no casualties, but it forced us to pack up all of our belongings and move to a different area of Abu—from that night on I had to do without a bed.

On 28AUG another battalion from the Iraqi Army arrived to relieve us.

The majority of my unit left on 31AUG, which required me to spend my last night at Abu Ghraib in one of the outer towers where I was accompanied by two Iraqi soldiers.

I convoyed out (hopefully for the last time) on 01SEP. Of course it didn't go as planned, the four guntrucks in my convoy team had to make multiple trips between Stryker and Abu—which resulted in me going over 30 consecutive hours without a wink of sleep. Near the end, I thought that I was going to pass out in the turret.

Fortunately nothing happened, the trips were uneventful. Which just goes to show that it's better to be lucky than good—of course, it's best to be both.

When all was said and done, I was in the last group of 24 soldiers to leave the "outpost."

Here's an article on the closing of Abu Ghraib that I came across in "The Stars and Stripes" (the overseas military newspaper). The last detainees were transported out over 6 weeks ago—but I guess with the press it's better late than never: http://www.contracostatimes.com/mld/cctimes/news/15374198.htm[11] [see Appendix I]

Now we're all back at Camp Stryker. The delay has resulted in a mission change. Since we now only have about 2 months left in our tour, we are no longer being sent down to Camp Bucca—instead we will remain here at Stryker, living in tents, and doing detainee operations at Camp Cropper (a new detention facility in Baghdad). Cropper and Stryker are actually connected to one another, so the commute won't be a problem.

Hope all is well. Talk to you later.
Mike

11. Nancy A. Youssef, "In a milestone, Abu Ghraib prison is empty, officials say," *McClatchy Newspapers*, August 2006.

09/16/2006
Iraq Update—09/15/2006

My platoon was assigned the job of Detainee Escort at Camp Cropper. This basically entails us taking the detainees to/from their living area (a.k.a., the compounds) over to various locations for scheduled appointments (e.g., the hospital, MI, visitation, etc.).

Camp Cropper is a much more consolidated facility than Abu Ghraib, so we are able to simply walk the detainees from one area to another. The only time we have to load them into vehicles is for moves to/from the flight line (for chopper/ plane rides), and even then we are still within the confines of the overall facility. So for the rest of our tour it is highly likely that we will remain completely "inside the wire."

My individual assignment is Escort Base, meaning that I remain in the office manning the radio and handling paperwork. I keep track of all detainee appointments for the facility, and direct escorts to the appropriate places at the necessary times. Only when we are running short handed (due to an influx of movements) do I actually have to leave the office to escort detainees myself. It's a pretty boring job. I work from 1300 to 0200 (13 hours), six days a week (Sunday is my day off).

I get along really well with everyone that I work with (a.k.a., my squad). Both my Squad Leader and Platoon Sergeant are extremely competent, they really have a firm grasp of what's important and what isn't—which seems to be extremely rare in the U.S. Army. For example, a soldier in one of the other platoons was caught by a senior-NCO walking from the latrine to the showers (about 15 ft.) with the back of his shirt inadvertently untucked—he was berated and made to perform 15 hours of extra-duty. That kind of nonsense is commonplace around here. Most of us can accept long hours and poor conditions, it's all of the little things like that which really kills morale.

As I mentioned in my last e-mail, we are living on Camp Stryker. Since we don't have much longer in our tour, they've stuck us in tents near the back of the FOB. My entire platoon (about 40 guys) is crammed into one tent, with our little nylon cots lined up in rows about 2 ft. from one another. We are living about a mile and a half away from the main portion of the post (where the phones, television, PX, DFAC, etc. are located).

I read a TIME magazine article from about 3 weeks ago that dubbed one of the roads where we used to frequently provide convoy security on as "The Highway of Death." I don't know who or how they come up with these little monikers, but over here we all find them pretty amusing.

Hope all is well. Talk to you later.
Mike

10/01/2006
Iraq Update—10/01/2006

It has been over a year since we left our loved ones for this deployment.

The time away has been very hard on many relationships in my unit. We've had four guys who have had to sign divorce papers during their 2-week leave, and at least twice that many have had engagements broken off. My unit has received dozens of "Dear John" letters. One of the younger soldier's girlfriend didn't even go through the trouble of writing a letter, she just mailed him a picture of her performing oral sex on another man—he was pretty upset about it.

In the Army we have a term to describe the guy who swoops in on a soldier's spouse/girlfriend while he's deployed: Jody. During Basic Training the Drill Sergeants spoke of him often: "Don't worry Private, Jody is taking good care of your girl!" It looks like Jody has kept himself very busy with some of the girls that this unit left behind.

I think one of the problems is a lack of social support for many of the families of deployed National Guard soldiers. In the active-duty Army, a soldier's family/friends live on or very near to a post filled with a community of people who are coping with the same experience. But in the National Guard, a significant other is simply given a phone number along with the vague instructions to "call if there are any problems." Loneliness cannot be solved with an 800 number.

Over 40% of the troops that served in Iraq last year were National Guardsman; and that's on top of all of our other missions: disaster relief (hurricanes, wild fires, etc.), the on-going Hurricane Katrina clean-up, state counter drug programs, Afghanistan, Mexican border operations, etc.

Since we also work in the civilian world, we possess a diversity of skill unlike any other branch of service. Some of the first up-armored Humvees in Iraq were designed and welded together with scrap metal by a deployed soldier who normally worked as an engineer; I know my computer skills definitely came in handy with the Internet at Abu Ghraib.

Hopefully the strain caused by the rapid increase in State/Federal activations won't permanently damage the National Guard. It's pretty clear that compensation will have to be increased to keep enlistments high enough to properly sustain our many missions. My term of enlistment is up in about a year, and since I'm not re-upping (I've done my part) I guess it'll soon be somebody else's problem.

There is a question that I've been asked a few times by some of you, and I'd be remiss if I failed to answer before leaving here: Are we winning the war in Iraq?

My answer is that we've already won our war: we've defeated the Iraqi Army, toppled the government, captured Saddam Hussein, killed al-Zarqawi, and oversaw the establishment of a representative democracy. What we are left with now (the violent clashes between Sunnis and Shias) is an ideological/political problem that can only be solved by the Iraqis themselves.

Currently, the American armed forces are assisting the new Iraqi govt. (which is less than 5 months old) in their efforts to secure/stabilize the country; but the sectarian violence is just a symptom of a larger problem: a lack of trust between the Sunnis and Shias—and as I've stated in the past, that problem cannot be solved with guns, it will require political compromise between the factions. Whether or not they will ultimately be successful still remains to be seen—but at this point it is almost entirely out of our hands.

Hope all is well. Talk to you later.
Mike

10/15/2006
Iraq Update—10/15/2006

I'm sorry that my e-mails have been less frequent lately. I'm having trouble motivating myself to do much of anything. I spend most of my time away from work crashed out on my cot watching movies. I just feel so worn down.

The battalion that my company has been under during our entire time in-country went back home, and a new battalion has rotated in. It appears that the new battalion didn't receive very much relevant training, because they have absolutely no idea what they're doing; and they refuse to seek counsel from those of us who are experienced in executing this assignment—instead they seem intent on proving that they are "in-charge" by proceeding in a manner of condescension and arrogance.

Our exit date keeps sliding back, which is frustrating. I feel kind of like a marathon runner who has paced himself perfectly for a certain distance, and collapses after crossing the finish-line only to discover that an extra lap has been unknowingly added to the race. Right now I'm just trying to eek out these last few steps.

My time in Iraq has definitely lengthened the list of items that I consider to be luxuries. Here are some of the little things that I'm looking foreword to leaving behind:

* Porta-johns, and getting hit by that gross blue splash.
* Having to wear shoes in the shower.
* Resting my weary body (and sore back) on an 1/8 inch of fabric that the Army calls a cot.
* Plastic knives/forks which constantly break and refuse to cut the KBR mystery meat served in the chow hall.

And of course the thousands of little things every day (how to speak, stand, dress, cut your hair, etc.) which come with the individual freedom that soldiers (property of the U.S. govt.) don't possess.

It's rained each of the past three days, hopefully we'll be out of here before it gets too much worse.

Hope all is well. Talk to you later.
Mike

10/25/2006
Iraq Update—10/25/2006

Our relieving unit has arrived, they are a National Guard company out of Illinois. It's fun watching them take their first steps. It seems like ages have passed since my initial arrival in Iraq; but I'm trying to remember back to when I was in their shoes, when things were still new and a little bit frightening. I know that eventually the daily grind turns even dramatic events into mundane routine, so I try not to roll my eyes when I hear them talk of things like the distant mortar-fire. I am glad that we were able to close Abu Ghraib (where the mortars weren't so distant) before they got here; their tour should be much more peaceful than ours has been.

As for my company, the count-down home is pretty much all that is on our minds. Talk of home dominates everyone's discussions; the content of conversations are what you'd expect from a bunch guys winding down 14 months of forced celibacy: 90% sex, 9% booze, with the remaining percent split between fishing and football.

But, some soldiers in my unit won't be consuming any alcoholic beverages for quite a while. Typically about a third of the soldiers who work in a detention facility over here end up contracting tuberculosis before the end of their tour. Those who are positive are required to take daily medication for nine months. The medicine can cause some fairly significant liver damage, so those consuming it are prohibited from drinking alcohol during their treatment.

On Saturday, I was injected with the tuberculosis test, and within a few hours that portion of my forearm developed a bright red rash; I thought for sure that I was positive for TB. Fortunately, over the next day the rash began to subside, and was virtually non-existent by Monday (when the medic checked the result). Not everyone was as lucky, a couple of soldiers in my squad (whom I work along side every day) ended up testing positive. Hopefully their treatment will go as smoothly as possible.

My company is scheduled to leave Iraq in the next 10 days. We'll spend a few days in Kuwait, and then fly to Ft. Stewart where it will take about a week to out-process (medical/psychological evaluations, paperwork, etc.). Then we will be bused back to our armory in Plant City and be officially released. I can't believe that this is all really almost over.

There are two common questions asked of returning war vets. To save you all the trouble, I'll answer them both now:

1. Did you kill anyone?
   No

2. What was your closest call with death?

I've had a few close calls, but the one I consider to be my closest came in early August. We were back from convoy, and I went into a tent to get out of the sun and cool down for a little while.

I wasn't in there 5 minutes when I heard a loud WHOOOOOSH!!! immediately followed by a THUD!! which shook the floor-boards and rattled the tent. When I went out to investigate, I found a deep hole near the back of the tent about 5 m from where I had been resting.

The hole had been created by a rocket that failed to detonate when it collided with the ground. If it hadn't been a dud, I would have been blown to pieces. I owe my life to a manufacturing defect—thank goodness for poor Soviet craftsmanship.

Hope all is well. Talk to you later.
Mike

10/31/2006
Iraq Update—Week 62

Intelligent and informed people can disagree on the causes and prudence of the conflict in Iraq. However, the unequivocal result is that a once-oppressed people will have the opportunity for liberty. Like all democracies, whether or not that opportunity materializes into a reality is ultimately in their own people's hands. Upon the conclusion of the U.S. Constitutional Convention in 1787, Benjamin Franklin was asked what type of government had been decided on, his response was: "A republic if you can keep it." The same is true for the Iraqis today.

We should look humbly at our own history (which includes slavery, civil war, reconstruction, robber barons, segregation, secret arrests, torture, etc.) before casting doubt and cynicism on the Iraqi people. They will make mistakes, and there will be regressions. No government is perfect, anything man-made will have flaws because human beings are flawed. The question every person—and nation—needs to ask themselves is: "Are we making progress?"

The U.S. Constitution is a flawed document, on its inception it protected the institution of slavery, but it was a huge leap forward in providing a model for representative government and the protection of individual rights. Yes initially only the individual rights of selected classes, races, and genders were protected, but the document provided the framework for those rights to be expanded to all. Freedom and liberty are a continual work in progress, and as we continue to develop intellectually the very meaning of those terms change. There is no finish line, there is always more work to be done.

America's great gift to the world is that we have constantly pushed ourselves toward progress, and we have demanded the same from others, sometimes in the face of great opposition. As Americans, we are not afraid to look at ourselves, admit our wrongs and correct them. We are also not afraid to look at our neighbors, explain to them why THEY are wrong, and help correct them as well.

I love America; and by that I don't mean that I love the dirt between the Atlantic and Pacific Ocean where I happened to be born. What I'm referring to is the principles for which we stand—our commitment to progress and human liberty. I share Benjamin Franklin's sentiment that: "Where liberty dwells, there is my country." Even though I was deployed to a foreign soil, by fighting for democracy and the advancement of liberty, I was fighting for my country; and those are principles worth fighting for. Abbie Hoffman, who fought for them in a much different way than myself, once stated:

> *Democracy is not something you believe in or a place to hang your hat, it's something you do. You participate. If you stop doing it, democracy crumbles.*

I am proud to have participated in the defense of democracy.

Since I'm leaving Iraq in a few days, this will most likely be my last e-mail update. I want to thank you for allowing me to share portions of my journey with you; writing these e-mails has been kind of therapeutic. I look forward to seeing you all very soon.

Talk to you later.
Mike

Michael Keller returned home on November 11, 2006. He was happily received by his family and friends.

APPENDIX A

Abu Ghraib prison

Wikipedia.org

The Abu Ghraib prison (also Abu Ghurayb) is in Abu Ghraib, an Iraqi city 32 km west of Baghdad. It became internationally known as a place where Saddam Hussein's government tortured and executed dissidents, and later as the site of torture and abuse of Iraqi suspects by the United States military that was publicised in a series of photographs published in American news media.

Under Hussein's Ba'ath government, it was known as Abu Ghraib Prison and had a reputation as a place of torture. It was sometimes referred to in the Western media as "Saddam's Torture Central". The prison was renamed after United States forces expelled the former Iraqi government, which had called it the Baghdad Central Confinement Facility (BCCF) or Baghdad Central Correctional Facility. In May of 2004, Camp Avalanche, a tent camp on the grounds of Abu Ghraib for security detainees, changed its name to Camp Redemption at the request of a governing council member.

The prison complex was built by British contractors in the 1960s, and covered 280 acres (1.15 km^2) with a total of 24 guard towers. The size of a small town, the area was divided into five separate walled compounds for different types of prisoners. Each block contained a dining room, prayer room, exercise area and rudimentary washing facilities. Cells contained up to 40 people in a space four metres by four. By the fall of the government in 2003 the five compounds were designated for foreign prisoners, long sentences, short sentences, capital crimes and "special" crimes.

Under Saddam Hussein

Under the government of Saddam Hussein the facility was under the control of the Directorate of General Security (Al-Amn al-Amm) and was the site of the torture and execution of thousands of political prisoners—up to 4000 prisoners are thought to have been executed there in 1984 alone. During the 1990s human rights organization Amnesty International documented repeated events where as many as several hundred inmates were executed in a single episode. These included hundreds executed in November 1996, and several hundred members of the Shi'a denomination killed in 1998 and 2001. Amnesty reported that it could not produce a complete picture of events at the prison due to government secrecy.

The section for political inmates of Abu Ghraib was divided into "open" and "closed" wings. The closed wing housed only Shi'ites. They were not allowed visitors or any outside contact.

Coalition prisoners were held and tortured in Abu Ghraib during the Gulf War, including the British Special Air Service patrol Bravo Two Zero.

In 2001 the prison is thought to have held as many as 15,000 inmates. Hundreds of Shi'a Kurds and Iraqi citizens of Iranian ethnicity had reportedly been held there incommunicado and without charges since the beginning of the Iran-Iraq War. Guards fed shredded plastic to prisoners. There are allegations that some of these detainees were subjected to experiments as part of Iraq's chemical and biological weapons program.

The prison was abandoned prior to the 2003 invasion of Iraq. An expansion project began in early 2002 that would add six new blocks to the prison. In October 2002, Saddam Hussein gave amnesty to most prisoners in Iraq. After the prisoners were released, the prison was left empty to be vandalized and looted. Almost all of the documents relating to prisoners were piled and burnt inside of prison offices and cells, leading to extensive structural damage.

Under the US-led coalition

One of a series of photos taken by U.S. soldiers of Iraqi prisoners in Abu Ghraib. The hooded prisoner had wires attached to both hands and his penis, and was reportedly told that he would be electrocuted if he fell off the box he was standing on; the wires were not actually electrified. Currently the site known as the Abu Ghraib prison is used by both the U.S.-led coalition occupying Iraq and the Iraqi government. The area of the facility known as "the Hard Site" is under the complete control of the Iraqi government and is used for housing convicted criminals. The Hard Site is best known from the abuse scandal pictures, the photos of which were all taken in Tier 1 of the complex. The remainder of the facility is occupied by the United States military. It serves as both a FOB (Forward Operating Base) and a detention facility. All detainees are housed in an area known as "Camp Redemption." The camp is divided into 5 security levels. This recently built (Summer of 2004) camp replaced the three level setup of Camp Ganci, Camp Vigilant and Tier 1.

The prison has been used as a detention facility, holding more than 7,000 people at its peak in early 2004. The current population, however, is much smaller. This is, in part, because the new Camp Redemption has a much smaller capacity than Camp Ganci alone had. Many detainees have been sent from Abu Ghraib to Camp Bucca for this reason. All people being held by the United States military are housed in Camp Redemption, some of which are alleged rebels, some alleged criminals. Convicted criminals are transferred to the Iraqi run Hard Site. While there are certainly people being held that are not guilty of the allegations, work is constantly under way to clear their names and have them released. It was the opinion of senior UK and US officials that the prison should be demolished as soon as possible, however this was overruled by the interim Iraqi Government.

It is operated by only one battalion, even though army doctrine calls for one battalion per 4,000 enemy soldiers. By contrast the High Value Detainee (HVD) Complex, Camp Cropper, maintains only about 100 detainees, and is also run by a single battalion.

In late April 2004, U.S. television news-magazine 60 Minutes II broke a story that had been taken from The New Yorker involving regular torture and humiliation of Iraqi inmates by a small group of U.S. soldiers. The story included photographs depicting the torture of prisoners, and resulted in a substantial political scandal within the U.S. and other coalition countries.

On April 20, 2004 Twelve mortars were fired on the prison by insurgents. Twenty-two detainees were killed and 92 wounded. The attack was viewed as either as an attempt to incite a riot or retribution for detainees cooperating with the United States.

In May 2004 the US-led coalition embarked on a prisoner release policy to try to reduce numbers to fewer than 2000. Despite numerous large releases and transfers to Camp Bucca, this goal has yet to be obtained due to the number of incoming detainees.

In a May 24, 2004 address at the U.S. Army War College in Pennsylvania, United States President George W. Bush announced that the prison would be demolished. On June 14 Iraqi interim President Ghazi Mashal Ajil al-Yawer indicated that he opposed this decision, and on June 21 U.S. military judge Col. James Pohl ruled that the prison was a crime scene and could not be demolished.

On April 2, 2005 the prison was attacked by between 40 and 60 insurgents. Between 20 and 44 Americans and 12 Iraqi prisoners were injured in the attack. In another battle the next day, several insurgents were killed and more than forty US soldiers and at least thirteen Iraqi prisoners injured. According to the US military, about fifty insurgents were injured and a few others killed. Al Qaeda has claimed responsibility for both of the strikes.

During the week ending August 27, 2005, nearly 1,000 detainees at the Abu Ghraib prison were released at the request of the Iraqi government.

On December 4, 2005, Reuters reported that according to John Pace, human rights chief for the United Nations Assistance Mission in Iraq (UNAMI), those held in Abu Ghraib prison were among an estimated 14,000 people imprisoned in violation of UN Resolution 1546. According to Pace,

"All [prisoners in Iraq] except those held by the Ministry of Justice are, technically speaking, held against the law because the Ministry of Justice is the only authority that is empowered by law to detain, to hold anybody in prison."

1. http://en.wikipedia.org/wiki/Wikipedia:Text_of_the_GNU_Free_Documentation_License

APPENDIX B

Meet the real butcher of Abu Ghraib prison

Telegraph.co.uk

Saad Abdul Amir has a special reason to be thankful that Saddam Hussein is under lock and key. If the dictator had still been in power, Saad would have been hard at work operating the gallows at Abu Ghraib prison, executing political prisoners and criminals as part of the "celebrations" for Saddam's birthday on April 28.

Instead, Saad has time to reflect on the 11 years he spent as a hangman who sent thousands to their deaths. In 1992 he was a taxi driver in love with a young woman he had picked up in his cab. When he heard about a job as a guard at Abu Ghraib prison, in a suburb of Baghdad, he decided to apply, calculating that a steady income would enable him to buy a home, propose and settle down.

But, by a cruel irony, he was picked by prison administrators to work as a hangman precisely because he had no family. It was a job that came with a threat: say no and face a long spell behind bars. Instead of policing the thousands of prisoners held in Saddam's most brutal jail, he was forced to become one of 12 hangmen working in the execution block, a squat building on edge of the compound.

"When I was picked for the job I felt as if I was going to faint, I was completely lost," he said. Now 48 years old, he is stooped, with a craggy, pitted face—a shadow of the man he was 12 years ago. As he spoke, he hugged the shadows in the corner of a hotel lobby and played with the frayed edges of his shirt, his eyes shaded by large, dark sunglasses, a baseball cap pulled low over his face.

"I saw people die in the army, but that was in battle. Being in charge of an execution was completely different. I couldn't sleep for two nights after I was told I must take the job and I haven't had a night of peace since then. I don't know how many executions I took part in, I have lost count, but there were thousands, between 100 and 150 each month."

Instead of finding himself financially better off, Saad's salary rarely rose above $10 a month. The bonus paid for Saddam's birthday and the commissions of $5 for each execution were pocketed by prison chiefs.

During the last decade of Saddam's rule, tens of thousands of his political opponents and common criminals passed through Abu Ghraib to the gallows, where a single yank of the hangman's lever opened trapdoors beneath the feet of two prisoners at a time.

The execution block worked like a well-oiled machine. Twice a week, on Wednesdays and Sundays, men and women personally condemned to death by the dictator were marched 30 yards from their filthy cells to the second floor.

The condemned would often have to spend weeks standing up in the "correction cells" before they were marched past a smiling mural of Saddam and up the ramp to the gallows. "They were tortured for several days," said Saad. "You could scarcely recognise their faces, they were so swollen."

Two nooses, with knots of cotton to press on the victim's Adam's apple and the back of his neck, were looped through hooks above metal scaffolding. Under the trapdoors, two men waited to hurry along the execution, yanking the swinging bodies to snap their necks.

The hangmen lived in seclusion, living in their own mess room, where they watched television and drank Arak, the powerful local spirit.

"We were given Arak to drink all day, maybe a bottle of Arak each. It was the only way I could live with what I was doing. We would check the roster to see which of us had to work the gallows and if it was me I'd start to drink. You could always tell who was going to work the gallows by how drunk he was. By the end of the day, I would be completely drunk, but I learned to work the machine even after a bottle of Arak."

Even in Abu Ghraib Saddam's obsession with closely managing every aspect of his dictatorship was evident. He personally signed the execution warrant for each of the prisoners and on special occasions, like his birthday, was known to watch the executions.

"He sent down an order and at noon the guards called out the prisoner's name and then their mother's name, to make sure there was no mistake. After each name, the guards read the same message from Saddam Hussein, 'God bless his soul', which means the prisoner was going to be hung. It was always written on a yellow piece of paper. Then the prisoner was taken down the corridor to another room and held there until sunset, when we would hang them. Saddam always insisted the executions took place after sunset."

Still haunted by memories of the execution block, Saad recalls the screams of the prisoners as they were led to the gallows. "I remember when one man refused to be taken from his cell and the guards had to beat him with a metal bar until he was unconscious. I remember hearing his screams. He could hardly stand when I put the rope around his neck and two guards had to hold his head.

"The last man I executed was in his forties. It was two years ago, but I remember it clearly. He was from an Islamic party against Saddam and he cried out for God for almost a minute after I threw the lever, until he was pulled down by his legs and his neck snapped."

Almost three-quarters of those who were hanged in Abu Ghraib were political prisoners. After death, their eyes and organs were removed and sent to medical schools and their bodies dumped in mass graves outside the execution block. Several hundred women convicted of murder or drug dealing were also executed.

Saddam's brutality was given free rein after the failed uprising in 1992, when hundreds of thousands of opponents were murdered or sentenced to death, and in the last stages of the war when Uday, his psychopathic son, ordered the execution of deserters and political prisoners. Ironically, it was Saddam's decision to commute thousands of death sentences in 1995 and 2001 that set free prisoners who Saad now fears are hunting him.

Out of work and living on handouts, he is now leading a solitary life with neither wife nor family, rarely leaving his small apartment in a down at heel part of Baghdad.

"I took that job instead of getting married and lost everything. Now I dream of escaping from Iraq and having a family, but I know it will never happen. Sometimes I even dream of being a sailor: I've never seen the sea, but I know it would make me forget everything. I just want to be on the ocean, away from everything that reminds me of Saddam."

APPENDIX C

21 December 2005

TO: CPT XXXXX, XXXXX MP CO Commander

SUBJECT: Geneva Convention relative to the treatment of detainees at XXXXX

Since our initial briefing here at XXXXX, it has been apparent that there are several inconsistencies between provisions specified in the Geneva Convention and the actual treatment of detainees.

It is my understanding that military leadership has deemed our conduct here at XXXXX to be governed by the Geneva Convention. Secretary of Defense Donald Rumsfeld has publicly stated that "the Geneva Convention applies to all prisoners held in Iraq." These statements have been reiterated by senior military officials including LtGEN Ricardo Sanchez, GEN John Abizaid, and GEN George Casey.

In the past, GEN Casey has stated that violations of the Geneva Conventions in Iraq were the result of "a complete breakdown of discipline" and not "indicative of our training or our values."

For several weeks, I have been attempting to acquire a copy of the XXXXX Standing Operating Procedure (SOP) so that I could confirm that these inconsistencies are not a part of documented proper procedure, but so far I have been unable to obtain a copy to review.

For your convenience, I have provided the following list of practices seen during the introductory SOP briefing and compound tour given to the soldiers of the XXXXX MP CO that may be inconsistent with the Geneva Convention (III) Relative to the Treatment of Prisoners of War (August 12, 1949):

Geneva Convention (III), Section I, Article 18 states:

> "All effects and articles of personal use, except arms, horses, military equipment and military documents, shall remain in the possession of prisoners of war ... effects and articles used for their clothing or feeding shall likewise remain in their possession"

In the Special Housing Unit (SHU) here, detainees are stripped of all personal effects. In Level I—IV facilities, detainees are allowed prayer rocks and personal copies of the Koran (if no writing is present), and are stripped of virtually all other personal effects. Detainees are clothed in US provided jumpsuits.

Geneva Convention (III), Section II, Chapter I, Article 21 states:

> Subject to the provisions of the present Convention relative to penal and disciplinary sanctions, prisoners of war may not be held in close confinement except where necessary to safeguard their health and then only during the continuation of the circumstances which make such confinement necessary.

Here, detainees are routinely held in the SHU (which is a close confinement facility) for reasons other than the safeguarding of their health, including for intelligence gathering purposes.

Geneva Convention (III), Section II, Chapter II, Article 25 states:

> Prisoners of war shall be quartered under conditions as favourable as those for the forces of the Detaining Power who are billeted in the same area.
>
> The foregoing provisions shall apply in particular to the dormitories of prisoners of war as regards both total surface and minimum cubic space, and the general installations, bedding and blankets.

In Level I-IV facilities at XXXXX, detainees are billeted in tents, with approximately 25 detainees per tent, and sleep on mats laid on the ground. Soldiers stationed at XXXXX are generally billeted in 1–4 person rooms inside of concrete buildings, and sleep either on cots or mattresses.

Geneva Convention (III), Section II, Chapter II, Article 28 states:

> Canteens shall be installed in all camps, where prisoners of war may procure foodstuffs, soap and tobacco and ordinary articles in daily use.

There are no canteens established for detainee use at XXXXX.

Geneva Convention (III), Section II, Chapter VI, Article 41 states:

> In every camp the text of the present Convention and its Annexes and the contents of any special agreement provided for in Article 6, shall be posted, in the prisoners' own language, in places where all may read them. Copies shall be supplied, on request, to the prisoners who cannot have access to the copy which has been posted

Here, the text of the Geneva Convention is not visibly posted (in any language) in the compounds.

Geneva Convention (III), Section V, Article 72 states:

> Prisoners of war shall be allowed to receive by post or by any other means individual parcels or collective shipments containing, in particular, foodstuffs, clothing, medical supplies and articles of a religious, educational or recreational character which may meet their needs, including books, devotional articles, scientific equipment, examination papers, musical instruments, sports outfits and materials allowing prisoners of war to pursue their studies or their cultural activities …
>
> The only limits which may be placed on these shipments shall be those proposed by the Protecting Power in the interest of the prisoners themselves, or by the International Committee of the Red Cross or any other organization giving assistance to the prisoners, in respect of their own shipments only, on account of exceptional strain on transport or communications.

Detainees at XXXXX are prohibited from receiving parcels or collective shipments.

Geneva Convention (III), Section VI, Chapter III, Article 89 states:

> The disciplinary punishments applicable to prisoners of war are the following:
>
> (1) A fine which shall not exceed 50 per cent of the advances of pay and working pay which the prisoner of war would otherwise receive under the provisions of Articles 60 and 62 during a period of not more than thirty days.

> (2) Discontinuance of privileges granted over and above the treatment provided for by the present Convention.
>
> (3) Fatigue duties not exceeding two hours daily.
>
> (4) Confinement.
>
> The punishment referred to under (3) shall not be applied to officers.
>
> In no case shall disciplinary punishments be inhuman, brutal or dangerous to the health of prisoners of war.

If a detainee in the SHU here commits a non-violent disciplinary infraction (such as reciting a prayer, or not showing proper respect to a guard), they are placed into a "restraint chair". The restraint chair has been found to be a primary or contributory cause of death in a number of cases across U.S. detention facilities. The United Nations Committee Against Torture issued recommendations to abolish the use of restraint chairs on the grounds that their use breaches the Convention against Torture and Other Cruel, Inhuman or Degrading Treatment. The United Nations Standard Minimum Rules for the Treatment of Prisoners stipulate that restraints should never be applied as a punishment.

Former Army SSG Ivan Frederick was court-martialed for "maltreatment of detainees" for an incident at Abu Ghraib in 2003 where he sat "on top of a detainee sandwiched in between two medical litters bound by padded material." In the SHU here, leaving detainees sandwiched in between two medical litters for periods exceeding an hour is also a routine punishment for disciplinary infractions.

<u>Geneva Convention (III), Section VI, Chapter III, Article 90 states:</u>

> The duration of any single punishment shall in no case exceed thirty days. Any period of confinement awaiting the hearing of a disciplinary offence or the award of disciplinary punishment shall be deducted from an award pronounced against a prisoner of war.
>
> The maximum of thirty days provided above may not be exceeded, even if the prisoner of war is answerable for several acts at the same time when he is awarded punishment, whether such acts are related or not.

At XXXXX, detainees are routinely kept in the SHU for periods greater than thirty days.

In the effort to ensure that there is no future "breakdown in discipline," I am requesting a copy of the SOP and would respectfully suggest that one be distributed to every soldier of the XXXXX MP CO as well.

Please know that I have a deep admiration for the honor, integrity, and professionalism of the soldiers with whom I serve. My only objective is to ensure that those attributes are not compromised because of a simple, avoidable misunderstanding of procedure. I am deeply honored to serve in the XXXXX MP CO, and under the XXXXX MP BN. XXXXX XXXXXX

Respectfully,

XXXXX X XXXXXX
SGT, XXXXX MP CO

APPENDIX D

28 December 2005

TO: LTC XXXXX, XXXXX MP BN Commander

SUBJECT: Geneva Convention relative to the treatment of detainees at XXXXX

ENCLOSED: (1) Letter to CPT XXXXX, 21 December 2005

I am deeply honored to serve under the XXXXX MP BN, and I genuinely hope this correspondence is well received.

It has been apparent since my arrival at XXXXX that there are several inconsistencies between provisions specified in the Geneva Convention and the actual treatment of detainees here. It is my understanding that military leadership has deemed our conduct here at XXXXX to be governed by the Geneva Convention.

For several weeks, I have attempted, unsuccessfully, to acquire a copy of the XXXXX Standing Operating Procedure (SOP) so that I could confirm that these inconsistencies are not a part of documented proper procedure. But for some reason, even upon request, the SOP is not available. I communicated this problem to my Company Commander CPT XXXXX in writing over a week ago, and he has yet to respond. I am therefore utilizing your "open door policy" to bring this issue directly to your attention.

You will find enclosed a letter to my Company Commander dated 21 December 2005 which contains a list of practices here at XXXXX that may be inconsistent with the Geneva Convention (III) Relative to the Treatment of Prisoners of War (August 12, 1949).

In the effort to ensure that U.S. policy is not violated as a result of a misunderstanding of procedure, I am requesting a copy of the SOP and would respectfully suggest it be widely distributed to the other soldiers serving under the XXXXX MP BN as well.

Respectfully,

XXXXX X XXXXX
SGT, XXXXX MP CO

APPENDIX E

An Iraqi detainee screams "Allah" while tied down in a "humane restraint chair" at Abu Ghraib Prison on October 28, 2005. U.S. Army military police said that the suspected insurgent, a juvenile, had been given two hours in the chair as punishment for disrespecting them. (Photo by John Moore/Getty Images)

APPENDIX F

APPENDIX G

Whistleblowers' stomach-curdling story: Halliburton serves contaminated water to troops

HalliburtonWatch.org
20 Sept. 2005

WASHINGTON, Sept. 20 (HalliburtonWatch.org)—Outrage overflowed on Capitol Hill this summer when members of Congress learned that Halliburton's dining halls in Iraq had repeatedly served spoiled food to unsuspecting troops. "This happened quite a bit," testified Rory Mayberry, a former food manager with Halliburton's KBR subsidiary.

But the outrage apparently doesn't end with spoiled food. Former KBR employees and water quality specialists, Ben Carter and Ken May, told HalliburtonWatch that KBR knowingly exposes troops and civilians to contaminated water from Iraq's Euphrates River. One internal KBR e-mail provided to HalliburtonWatch says that, for "possibly a year," the level of contamination at one camp was two times the normal level for untreated water.

"I discovered the water being delivered from the Euphrates for the military was not being treated properly and thousands were being exposed daily to numerous pathogenic organisms," Carter informed HalliburtonWatch.

Carter worked at Camp Ar Ramadi, located 70 miles west of Baghdad in the notoriously violent Sunni Triangle, but he says water contamination problems exist throughout Iraq's military camps. He helped manage KBR's Reverse Osmosis Water Purification Unit (ROWPU), which is a water treatment system designed to produce potable (drinkable) water from a variety of raw water sources such as lakes, lagoons and rivers. ROWPU is supposed to provide the troops with clean water from Iraq's Euphrates River.

William Granger of KBR Water Quality for Iraq reached this conclusion in an e-mail after investigating Carter's complaint: "Fact: We exposed a base camp population (military and civilian) to a water source that was not treated. The level of contamination was roughly 2x the normal contamination of untreated water from the Euphrates River." Granger admitted that the contamination was "most likely ... ongoing through the entire life" of the camp, but that he was "not sure if any attempt to notify the exposed population was ever made."

In a company e-mail last March to his superior, Harold "Mo" Orr, coordinator for Halliburton's health and safety department said, "We have determined that the military (Command Surgeon) has not given any kind of signoff on the military ROWPU (As required by the military SOP) nor has KBR ever inquired about this before. This was only discovered thru the investigation of possible contamination by Ben Carter who is right now in charge of the ROWPU."

Orr's request for further investigation into the matter was overruled by KBR's health, safety and environmental manager, Jay Delahoussaye, who said in an e-mail that the initial health hazard turned out to be "erroneous" and that "corrective measures" were taken and "No KBR personnel were exposed to contaminated water."

But Granger responded with another e-mail, saying it was unclear whether corrective action had been taken. He said it was "highly likely" that someone from KBR finally started chlorinating the water this year, but that "there is no documentation" to confirm it. Nor is there documentation to show KBR is testing the water three times per day as required by the military, Granger said.

Nonetheless, Carter said chlorination is not enough to remedy the problem since raw sewage is routinely dumped less than two miles from the water intake location, in violation of military policy and procedure. "Chlorination of water tanks, while certainly beneficial, is not sufficient protection from parasitic exposure," Carter said in an e-mail to Granger, who is still employed with KBR.

According to Carter, Granger had written a scathing, 21-page report to KBR management about water quality at Ar Ramadi. Carter says the report proves the company's "incompetence and willful negligence" in protecting the water supply.

Granger has refused to comply with a company gag order and is convinced his employment will be terminated soon, says Carter. In an e-mail to Ken May, Granger said, "I stand by all of my e-mail's (internal or not). I have consistently been dogged in my approach that protection of the soldier, contractor, and subcontractor is paramount." In another e-mail to Carter, Granger said he would support Carter's legal actions and that he's looking into legal protections for himself as a whistleblower. "I won't turn over any documents until I understand what is protected or not ... but know that if called to testify or such that I will disclose all that is in the report verbally," he said in the e-mail.

Carter is in the process of obtaining worker's compensation from Halliburton over an illness he says was caused by the contaminated water.

Soldiers are often evacuated out of Iraq for non-combat related illnesses. The Association of Military Surgeons found that 9.1 percent of soldiers evacuated in 2003 suffered from problems of the digestive system; another 6.4 percent had nervous system disorders; 6.1% suffered urological problems; and 8.3 percent suffered from unknown illnesses.

In the early months of the war, the Army sent a team of investigators to probe a series of mysterious illnesses. Earlier this month, Canada reported an outbreak of gastrointestinal problems among soldiers serving in Afghanistan, where KBR is also involved.

Halliburton spokesperson, Melissa Norcross, told HalliburtonWatch that the water contamination allegations are "unfounded" and that "KBR has conducted its own inspection of the water at the site in question and has found no evidence to substantiate the allegations made by these former employees."

Norcross confirmed that non-potable (non-drinkable) water "was produced" at Ar Ramadi at the time of the camp's inception until May 2005, but that the military approved its use for showering and doing laundry. "During that time, bottled water was used for drinking and food preparation," she said.

Carter and May agree that KBR supplies bottled water for drinking, but that it's "absolutely untrue" that it's used for food preparation. Moreover, they never observed any posted signs or notices informing personnel not to drink the tap water, a possible sign of corporate negligence.

Of a possible sign of things to come, May said he observed an unsecured potable water tank used for food preparation at a dining facility. The bolts used to tighten the lid over the tank were missing. In an e-mail to HalliburtonWatch, May said the tank was located in an open area "for anyone to enter, including the enemy." He worries that "contaminants/poisons could be introduced which could result in mass casualties."

Additionally, May said he and another KBR employee witnessed water being filled through an open lid on top of the water tank, thereby rendering the once potable water as non-potable. "Water is required to be pumped into the tank through a male/female hose hook-up with no direct exposure to the air," May said. Failure to do so would result in exposing the camp population to non-potable water. May and Carter say they notified KBR's quality assurance and quality control department, including Chief of Services Warren Smith, but no remedial action was taken.

Today, Norcross says KBR supplies clean drinking water throughout Camp Ar Ramadi, but that "For drinking and food preparation, KBR continues to supply bottled water throughout Iraq." She insists that "there have been no documented cases of unusual illnesses or health conditions" at Ar Ramadi.

But a private company e-mail supplied to HalliburtonWatch appears to conflict with Halliburton's public denial. Halliburton public relations official, Jennifer Dellinger, wrote to her colleagues that Faith Sproul, who works in Halliburton's workers' compensation department, "does believe that initial tests showed some contamination to be present." As a result, Dellinger wrote, Sproul was concerned that former employees might "make a claim for disability" and "we could receive some queries on this if these former employees decide to go to the press." So, Dellinger asked her public relations colleagues, "Can you run some traps on this and see what you can find out?"

When HalliburtonWatch asked about this internal e-mail and its apparent confirmation of Carter and May's allegations, Norcross responded by saying the e-mail was written last July, prior to the company's final determination that no contamination occurred.

Carter resigned two weeks prior to Ken May, discovering what he said was "unsafe water and pressure to cover it up." "I tried to correct the problem, only to be blackballed by management and I eventually left this employment," Carter told HalliburtonWatch. Carter and May cite "poor company behavior patterns and practices from Site Management as the tell-tale sign of disaster looming around the corner if intervention is not taken very soon."

KBR's health and safety manager at Ar Ramadi, Harold Orr, also resigned because of the water issue but has remained silent, says May.

Carter and May also describe instances where a site manager urged everyone to conceal contamination information from the company's health and safety department. According to May, statements were made in an "All Hands Meeting" by then Site Manger Suzanne-Raku Williams, Warren Smith, and acting Medic Phillip Daigle suggesting that if anyone became sick, it was probably from the handles from the port-a-lets toilets and not from water contamination. In response, Ken May resigned out of disgust and frustration. In an e-mail to superiors, he chastised KBR for what he said was "retaliatory behavior from dishonest site management" and "inaction" that "compromised" camp safety and the health of the people who work there. He expressed concern over "the lack of oversight from the outside to investigate, redirect, and periodically monitor" the water to assure a healthy workplace. "Unfortunately, because of the lack of regards for my wellbeing [and] no response or action from KBR/Halliburton I have no recourse other than to resign," he said in an e-mail to his supervisor.

Carter and May's experience is not uncommon at KBR, where former employees have described instances of being ostracized or terminated if they dare to speak out against company negligence, mismanagement or malfeasance. Other former KBR employees have testified about being fired or urged to quit or conceal information after pointing out low-cost solutions to simple problems. But, a cynic might note, allowing small problems to grow into expensive ones through purposeful neglect actually boosts KBR's profits as there is a profit guarantee of 1% to 3% over cost for the LOGCAP III contract. As with all of KBR's "cost plus" military contracts, the more expensive the problem, the greater the fee paid to KBR from the government. So, it would seem there is actually a built-in incentive not to prevent small problems or reward whistleblower employees like Carter and May when neglect will result in a costlier problem down the road and more profits for KBR.

Update: The Senate Democratic Policy Committee held hearings on the water contamination issue on January 23, 2006.

APPENDIX H

I am the gunner for Cobra 11 Delta Team 652 MP Co. On 22JUL06, my guntruck was part of a convoy escorting 20 KBR trucks from FOB Abu Ghraib to BIAP.

At approx 0943, we were actively engaged by small arms fire on MSR Tampa just west of MSR Yankees. After hearing approx a seven round burst of fire, I informed my Team Chief SGT Herren that we were receiving fire from the 0300 position. I then heard a second burst of approx seven rounds.

Being unable to clearly identify the muzzle flash, IAW ROE I continued to scan my sector while refraining from returning fire. The driver SPC Doherty drove our vehicle out of harms way, and we continued on to complete our objective.

SGT Michael Keller

APPENDIX I

In a milestone, Abu Ghraib prison is empty, officials say

U.S. officials moved 3,600 detainees recently; Iraqi troops guard facility until government decides what to do with the site

By Nancy A. Youssef
McCLATCHY NEWSPAPERS

BAGHDAD, Iraq—The infamous prison at Abu Ghraib, scene of an abuse scandal that tarnished the United States' reputation worldwide and helped to fuel the growth of Iraq's insurgency, is now empty, Iraqi government officials have told McClatchy Newspapers.

The officials said U.S. authorities finished moving about 3,600 prisoners from the prison in recent days. Most went to one of two U.S.-run detention centers—Camp Cropper, near Baghdad International Airport, and Camp Bucca near Umm Qasr in southern Iraq. Some were released, according to one official, who works for the Ministry of Human Rights.

Defense Minister Hashem Shebli confirmed Saturday that the prison is now vacant and that Iraqi army troops have been assigned to help guard the facility, which frequently has been the target of insurgent mortar fire.

Lt. Col. Keir-Kevin Curry, a U.S. military spokesman for Detainee Operations, acknowledged that the United States had been moving prisoners but wouldn't say if the task had been completed. "This transfer will allow us to consolidate our effort at fewer sites and improve the conditions for both the coalition guards and the detainees," he said.

The emptying of the prison marks a milestone for the huge stone structure whose name has long been synonymous with torture, first under the regime of Saddam Hussein, then under American occupation when photos surfaced in April 2004 of U.S. troops abusing Iraqi prisoners there.

Eventually seven low-level soldiers were convicted of various charges, and the reserve general in charge of the facility was demoted and dismissed. A lieutenant colonel who oversaw the interrogation center was charged in the case only this past April, two years after the scandal broke.

But the Abu Ghraib abuse's greatest impact was no doubt symbolic. Many analysts believe the scandal helped draw recruits to Iraq's anti-American insurgency and helped fuel anti-American sentiment among Muslims throughout the world.

In June, Iraqi officials moved their 3,800 prisoners—mostly those convicted in Iraqi court—and placed them in prisons throughout the capital, Shebli said.

What happens next is unclear. U.S. authorities are securing the compound, several Iraqi officials said, and will eventually transfer it to Iraqi forces. Iraqi officials said that could be months away. None of the Iraqis would speak for the record because no official announcement has been made.

The Iraqi government is debating what to do then. Some believe the facility should be turned into a museum that remembers those who suffered there while others believe it should be torn down. Others rejected that, saying the government cannot afford to build a new prison.

Shebli said he does not believe the Iraqi government is prepared to use Abu Ghraib to hold prisoners without U.S. help. "We will take more courses on how to deal with prisoners in a more humane way," he said.

Ali Debaugh, a spokesman for Prime Minister Nouri Maliki, said the government still hasn't decided what it will do with the prison and does not have a timeline for when it will.

Built in the 1960s by British contractors, the facility began as a normal prison, designed to hold a few thousand. But during Saddam's regime, the facility's population ballooned to 50,000. In some areas of the facility, there were torture chambers and Saddam and his sons were said to regale in watching the tortured death of some of their more hated citizens.

After the war, several mass graves were found at the site.

Under U.S. control, the facility held as many as 15,000 inmates. And the prison has never shaken its reputation from the 2004 scandal, despite major reforms by U.S. officials.

978-0-595-45605-5
0-595-45605-7

Printed in the United Kingdom
by Lightning Source UK Ltd.
124986UK00002BA/272/A

9 780595 456055